MURDER IN THE HEARTLAND

JAY DIX, MD

*Medical Examiner, Boone and Callaway Counties, Missouri
Associate Professor of Pathology, University of Missouri*

WITH

JOE MOSELEY
*Past Prosecuting Attorney for
Boone County, Missouri*

ROBERT AHSENS
*Assistant Attorney General,
State of Missouri*

Murder in the Heartland, Copyright 2000

Published by AIS (Academic Information Systems)

5609 St. Charles Rd., Columbia, Missouri, 65202

ISBN # 0-9663422-3-2

All rights reserved

Printed in the United States of America

9 8 7 6 5 4 3 2

This book is dedicated to my wife and partner, Mary.

Contents

Preface   *vii*

CASE 1   Murder of a Wife   1

CASE 2   Murder of a Child   33

CASE 3   Murder in the Convenience Store   69

CASE 4   Murder of a Family   113

References   *149*
About the Author   *151*

Preface

Murder has always been a topic that has fascinated mankind. This is especially true for those of us who deal with murder cases on a day-to-day basis. Throughout my career I have been intrigued by the many different kinds of evidence that connect a killer to his victim. Over the years, I have found one thing to be true: it takes teamwork to put the puzzle pieces together to solve the problem of who committed the crime. Many individuals, regardless of their experience, training, and background, must work together in order to bring the murderer to justice.

Each of the four murders described in this book was a real murder case which occurred in Mid-Missouri. All the facts and details included herein are based on actual court documents, police reports, and autopsy results. In one case that follows, the investigators discover the essential evidence that proves the guilt of the assailant, while in another, the pathologist unearths important clues about the injuries. DNA holds the key in yet another case as the experts identify blood that belongs to the victim even though the body is never found. Every case is discussed from the time the victim is noticed missing or the body is discovered to the final verdict.

JD

CASE 1

Murder of a Wife

THE MISSING SPOUSE

Ralph Davis, an insurance salesman, lived with his wife, Susan, and their two children, Angela and Robbie, at 1300 Obermiller Road, in Columbia, Missouri. They had been married since 1979. Robbie was born in 1977 and Angela was born in 1982.

In November, 1985, Susan briefly moved out of the house with her children and stayed at the home of a friend; she filed a petition for dissolution of marriage from Ralph on November 16, but dismissed the petition two weeks later. She later told her attorney that her husband had threatened to physically harm her if she did not dismiss the petition. Early in 1986, Susan telephoned a local minister, David Ballenger, and asked him to come to their house because she and her husband were continuing to have serious marital problems. She wanted him to take custody of all their firearms and have a talk with Ralph, saying that she was concerned about Ralph's "welfare." Ballenger arrived, spoke to Ralph, and took two rifles, a shotgun, and a handgun with him as he left.

On May 19, 1986, a criminal charge was filed against Ralph in the Circuit Court of Boone County for assault in the third degree against his wife. The same day, Susan filed an adult abuse action against Ralph. The judge issued an order of protection that restrained Ralph from being on the premises of the home, and Susan was awarded temporary custody of the children. Ralph was arrested on the assault charge and served with the *ex parte* order that same day. He was allowed to post a cash bond on the condition that he have no contact with his wife. Meanwhile, Susan Davis and her children fled Columbia to find refuge with her parents in Iowa; she clearly considered her husband to be dangerous.

Beginning on the day the order of protection and bond were issued, and for some ten days thereafter, Ralph repeatedly violated the orders of the court by returning to the house on Obermiller Road. He admitted to a neighbor, John Holste, that he knew he was violating the order of protection and asked Holste not to contact the police (Figs. 1.1 and 1.2).

On Monday, June 2, a hearing was held in the Associate Circuit Court of Boone County on the adult abuse petition filed by Susan Davis. She came back from Iowa to be present at the hearing with Ralph. By agreement of both parties, a full order of protection required Ralph to restrain for 180 days from abusing his wife or entering their residence. Susan went back to Iowa immediately after the hearing, but returned to Columbia in order to keep her job as a secretary with Westinghouse Corporation. According to family and friends, she planned to re-establish her work, satisfy herself that it was safe to live at home, and then return to Iowa on June 13 to retrieve the children.

On the afternoon of June 5, Susan learned from her neighbor, John Holste, that Ralph had been at their residence in violation of the *ex parte* order of protection. As John and Susan stood talking at the door, Ralph appeared, and Susan excitedly said, "Oh my God, there he is. I've got to get out of here." Susan attempted to flee, but Ralph confiscated her car keys and grabbed her by the hair, saying he just wanted to talk to her. As they struggled, Holste advised Ralph he was going to call the sheriff and then went inside to do so. Ralph followed his neighbor into the house and attempted to keep him from using the

CASE 1 — MURDER OF A WIFE

FIGURE 1.1 Susan Davis. Her photograph was taken at the police station shortly after being physically abused by her husband.

FIGURE 1.2 Ralph Davis. This is his arrest photograph.

telephone. Unsuccessful in this effort, Davis ran out of the house and sped away in his car. Due to Holste's phone call, police officers arrived at the scene to interview Susan, search the house, and make sure Ralph was no longer present. They found the car keys Ralph had taken from Susan on the floor of Holste's garage.

That same evening, Ralph returned to Holste's home with Minister David Ballenger. Ralph admitted to Holste that he had no money and no place to stay. Holste suggested to Ralph that if he turned himself in at that time, he would pay for his bond. But Ralph decided to turn himself in later, after he called the sheriff's office and discovered that a warrant had not been issued for him on the most recent assault. He begged Holste for three hundred dollars for temporary living expenses, and Holste gave him one hundred in cash.

On the following day, June 6, new criminal charges were filed against Ralph for the third-degree assault of his wife and for violation of the full order of protection. Ralph was arrested that day, and he posted a bond. The same day, a warrant was issued for Ralph on the previous assault charge, which had been filed on May 21, for violating the condition of the bond that he have no contact with Susan, However, this arrest warrant was not executed until four days later on June 10.

As of June 6, Ralph was charged with three misdemeanor offenses, each carrying a sentence of up to one year in the county jail. Knowing that she was the principal witness in each case, Susan made extensive efforts to avoid further contacts with Ralph. With the help of a friend from work, Alex Palmer, she changed the locks on her house and installed other devices to prevent outside entry through the garage door and windows. In Iowa, Susan bought a German Shepard which she brought home to Columbia for further protection. In her car, she kept a ten-pound fire extinguisher to defend herself if she were attacked. Susan clearly felt her life was in danger, and she left her children in Iowa for their protection.

The next Monday, June 9, Susan resumed her secretarial job. That same day, at 1:00 p.m., Ralph was arraigned on the charges filed the

CASE 1 — MURDER OF A WIFE

previous Friday for violation of the protection order and third-degree assault. Sometime between 2:00 p.m. and 6:00 p.m. Ralph purchased a 12-gauge shotgun and ammunition at the Bass Pro Shop in Columbia.

Between 6:00 and 6:30 p.m., Susan left work at the end of her regular shift, driving her car, a red, 1985 Ford Escort. She told Alex Palmer she was going straight home. Around 8:30 or 9:00 p.m., Alex telephoned Susan at her home to check on her. There was no answer. Susan Davis was never heard from again.

The next day, June 10, when Susan did not appear for work, Alex Palmer drove to Susan's house and then telephoned Susan's mother to express concern about her disappearance. Susan's mother telephoned the sheriff's office and reported her missing. On June 11, a deputy sheriff entered the house on Obermiller Rd. in response to the report that she was missing. There were no signs that Susan had intended to depart. Her clothes, luggage, prescription drugs and personal effects appeared to be present and undisturbed. Susan's dog was locked in the garage and had not recently been cared for. A television guide in the living room was open to listings for Sunday, June 8.

Susan was known to have worshiped her children, and she had a very close relationship with her adoptive mother. In fact, she normally telephoned her mother at least once each day. However, Susan never contacted her mother or her children after June 9. As a result of these and other discoveries, police used computer networks to begin a nationwide search for traces of Susan and her car. Neither was found.

Ralph filed for divorce against his wife on June 11, one day after her disappearance. Three days later he drove to Iowa and forced Susan's parents to surrender custody of the children. When he and the children returned to Columbia, they moved back into the house on Obermiller Road. As a result of Susan's disappearance, the three criminal charges previously filed against Ralph were dismissed because the major witness could no longer testify. Later, Ralph was granted a default divorce in which he was awarded the custody of his children and Susan was ordered to pay child support.

At the time of Susan's disappearance, Ralph was in serious debt. He admitted as much to his neighbor, John Holste. Tax records indicated that his personal income in 1986 was $3,359. During the previous six years, Ralph and Susan had accepted nearly $100,000 in gifts and loans from Susan's parents. Ralph was aware of the existence of a trust fund set up by Susan's grandparents which would bequeath $500,000 to Susan or to the children if anything happened to her. Ralph knew he would be in control of the money if the children inherited the money.

Over the next 20 months Ralph's actions became increasingly suspicious. He made a number of contradictory statements to friends, acquaintances and police regarding the whereabouts of Susan and her car. He stated at various times he didn't know where Susan and the car were or that Susan had driven to Texas to be with a boyfriend. He asked one of his employees to look for Susan's car while he was on the road selling insurance. At the same time, he forged Susan's name on checks from her checking account. In June and July of 1986, Ralph signed Susan's name on three of her personal checks in amounts totaling $900 dollars, two of which were honored by the bank. He also signed her name on a form removing her as beneficiary on his life insurance policy.

The first breakthrough in the case of Susan's disappearance occurred on March 7, 1988. Susan's car was discovered in the Apache-U-Store-It facility 30 miles away from Columbia in Jefferson City. The person renting the garage-sized unit had stopped paying the rental charges. The signature on the rental contract was that of Ralph Davis. The storage owner finally decided to open the unit and sell what he could to recoup the overdue payments. Inside the unit, the owner found Susan's red Escort. He called Ford Motor Company to check for a lien on the vehicle. This call triggered a call from Ford to the Boone County Sheriff's Department. The sheriff's department had arranged to be called if anyone inquired about the car from Ford. This discovery was essential to the case, because if the car had not been found, Ralph Davis would never have been brought to trial for murdering his wife (Figs. 1.3–1.5).

CASE 1 — MURDER OF A WIFE

FIGURE 1.3 Susan's car was discovered in The Apache-U-Store-It facility in Jefferson City, Missouri.

FIGURE 1.4 The car was discovered March 7, 1988, in one of those large storage units.

FIGURE 1.5 Susan Davis' Ford Escort was gathering dust for 20 months in the facility.

INVESTIGATION AFTER DISCOVERING THE CAR

After investigators took many photographs, the Ford Escort was transported to Columbia for processing. The driver's side window was shattered and plastic covered the opening. The inside of the car contained abundant glass fragments, a few shotgun pellets, and 31 fragments of what appeared to be bone. There were also three air freshener containers. Fragments of material which appeared to be dried tissue were especially prominent above and on the visors. The front windshield was broken, apparently by the rearview mirror impacting the glass. A dark material, thought to be blood, covered the carpet. A cut into the passenger seat revealed that abundant blood had soaked into the foam padding. There were paper towels in the car and some of the dried tissue appeared smeared, as if someone had attempted to clean it up. Inspectors retained all of the bone fragments, shotgun pellets, glass, dried tissue, and numerous samples of the carpet for analysis. The entire car was processed. In fact, everything in the car was removed and preserved as evidence (Figs. 1.6–1.14).

FIGURE 1.6 The driver's side window was covered with plastic because the glass had been shattered with a shotgun.

FIGURE 1.7 The smeared area (arrow) revealed someone had attempted to clean the car.

FIGURE 1.8 Three air fresheners were discovered in the car. The storage facility owner remembered Ralph buying them at the same time he bought a lock for the storage unit's door.

FIGURE 1.9 There was abundant dried material above and on the visors. This material was later identified as human tissue; however, it could not be matched to Susan.

FIGURE 1.10 The front windshield was broken by the rearview mirror. Susan's head probably struck the mirror after she was shot.

FIGURE 1.11 Abundant glass fragments, 31 pieces of bone, and shotgun pellets were found on the floor.

CASE 1 — MURDER OF A WIFE

FIGURE 1.12 Most of the glass and bone fragments were concentrated in the area between the door and the seat.

FIGURE 1.13 Blood was dried on the passenger seat and the carpet. Samples were collected and sent to a laboratory for DNA testing.

FIGURE 1.14 Specks of tissue were on the passenger's door. A shotgun pellet was discovered inside the door panel.

The manager of the storage facility remembered the day Ralph brought the car to be stored, but she was unable to identify Ralph from a photographic lineup. She recalled Ralph saying he needed a space large enough for a car and that he wanted to store the car to keep his wife from gaining possession of it in divorce proceedings. The manager specifically remembered that Ralph was perspiring heavily, and he asked to use the bathroom because he had an upset stomach. Her memory of the events was enhanced by her fear that her boss would be upset because she allowed a black man to use the facility's bathroom. Ralph bought a padlock from a nearby store to secure the unit since the facility didn't furnish locks. He also bought air fresheners to place in the car.

After leaving the car in the unit, Ralph called a taxi to take him back to Columbia. Investigators located the taxi driver who remembered Ralph Davis. The driver recalled Ralph telling him about needing to store the car because of upcoming divorce proceedings, and he remembered Ralph being agitated at the time he made the statement. The driver dropped Ralph off halfway between Jefferson City and Columbia because he only had enough money to cover 15 miles of the trip.

Law enforcement officials interviewed Ralph on March 8, the day after the discovery of the car. When asked about the car prior to learning of its discovery, Ralph said he hadn't seen either Susan or her car since June 5, 1986, the day he confronted her at the home of John Holste, his neighbor. He told a different story after he was shown the storage rental contract and was told Susan's car had been discovered. He said his wife came to his office and announced she was leaving him. When he laughed at her, she threatened him with a pistol. She was holding the pistol in one hand and her car keys in the other. He grabbed the keys from her hand, went outside to her car and started to drive away. According to Ralph, he had paid for the car and he wasn't going to let her take it. He clearly believed that Susan might not leave him if she didn't have a car. He finished his story by explaining that as he was driving away, Susan ran up to the driver's side of the car, smashed her hand and gun through the driver's side window, and cut herself so severely that some of her blood dripped inside the car. After this new version of the story, Ralph was placed under arrest for murder in the second degree.

Following the interview and arrest, a search of Ralph's business office revealed some new evidence. Investigators found Susan's diamond ring in his desk. The ring was identified by her mother as a ring from a previous marriage that she rarely removed and a co-worker remembered her wearing it on the day she disappeared. In the office trash can was a torn, overdue bill from Apache-U-Store-It for rent on the unit (Fig. 1.15). Also in Ralph's desk were the keys to Susan's car. This evidence indicated to investigators that Ralph had been with Susan the day of her disappearance. Investigators also conducted a

CASE 1 — MURDER OF A WIFE   15

search of Ralph's home. They discovered a shotgun matching the description of the gun sold to Ralph on the same day Susan disappeared and a box of shotgun shells containing #4 shot in the bedroom.

Dr. Sam Stout, a forensic anthropologist at the University of Missouri-Columbia, performed an examination of the 31 fragments of bone found in the car. He examined the fragments both with the naked eye and under the microscope. He also prepared microscopic sections to study the makeup of the bone. In his opinion, the bones were of human origin and most likely facial bones. When he fluoresced the bones, he saw rings around the structures called osteons. This yellow fluorescent pattern occurs when a person has taken the antibiotic tetracycline or a drug in the same family. Susan Davis had filled a prescription for tetracycline within two months prior to her disappearance. She used tetracycline as a treatment for acne. Evidence was

FIGURE 1.15 A torn bill for the storage rental unit was found in Ralph's office. Susan's diamond ring was in his desk.

mounting that the bone fragments found in the Ford Escort belonged to Susan Davis (Figs. 1.16 and 1.17).

Dr. Stout also noticed a gray smudge on one of the bone fragments. This material was sent to a laboratory at the University of Missouri for analysis. Scanning electron microscopy revealed the material to contain lead and antimony. These were the same elements that were present in the shotgun pellets discovered in the car. The pellets were a #4 shot, the same size as the pellets investigators discovered in the shells removed from Ralph's home.

The tissue from the car's visors was analyzed by the highway patrol crime lab in Jefferson City. Technicians found the substance to be human tissue, but it couldn't be classified any further because there was no DNA available for testing. The material on the carpet, which

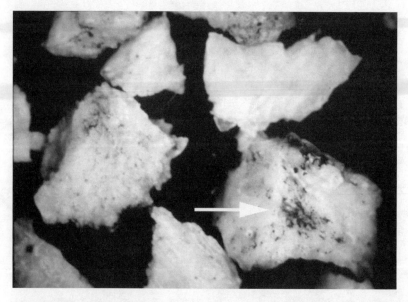

FIGURE 1.16 One of the 31 bone fragments discovered in the car was smudged with grey material (arrow). This material was found to have a similar makeup to the shotgun pellets from the car.

appeared to be blood, was proven to be human blood. It was saved for further DNA testing.

A forensic pathologist, Dr. Jay Dix, rendered an opinion based on the finding of the blood, bone and pellets found in the car. He stated that a shotgun blast to the face which resulted in the amount of blood seen in the car would have caused death. Even though no body was discovered or examined, he believed someone died in the car. Now the prosecution had to prove the blood in the car belonged to Susan Davis.

At the time of Susan's disappearance, the Missouri State Highway Patrol laboratory did not have the equipment and expertise to perform DNA testing. Cellmark Diagnostics Laboratory in Germantown, Maryland was one of a few labs that would accept specimens from around the country. The dried blood from the car was sent to Cellmark.

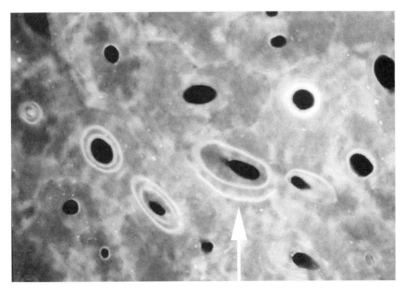

FIGURE 1.17 Seen under the microscope, these ring structures (arrow) indicated the decedent was taking the antibiotic tetracycline. Susan had been taking tetracycline for acne at the time of her disappearance.

In order to prove the blood in the car was Susan's, prosecutors needed comparative proof. The most common procedure would be to compare a known blood sample from Susan Davis with the sample from the car. Unfortunately, no blood sample known to be Susan's was available. The next most common method would be through paternity testing. That is, blood from her parents could be compared to hers and a positive identity could be made.

A person's genetic make-up is determined by his or her parents, so all of the properties of that person's DNA would be found in the DNA of at least one of the parents. But this approach was not available to authorities in this case because Susan was adopted and her natural parents were unknown. Therefore, reverse paternity testing had to be performed.

Samples of blood from Susan's children and her husband were tested to determine if the blood in the car was that of the mother of the children. By comparing the results from the testing of the four samples, it could be determined whether or not the blood in the car came from the mother of the children. The procedure would involve first comparing the results from the father's test and eliminating all of the DNA properties identical to those in the children's results. If the DNA properties which remained in the children's genetic make-up were present in the DNA from the car, then that blood came from the mother. Blood was taken from Ralph by a court order. Samples from Robbie and Angela Davis, in addition to Ralph Davis, were sent to Cellmark Laboratories.

The results from Cellmark were favorable to the state's case. The laboratory expert who performed the DNA test reported that the blood in the car was that of the mother of the two children, Robbie and Angela Davis.

Further interviews with witnesses divulged threatening comments made by Ralph prior to his wife's disappearance. In a series of conversations with his neighbor, John Holste, during the time Susan was in Iowa, Ralph stated he and his wife had been having marital problems for some time. He said Susan had been having affairs and doing drugs. He also told John the only way to "stop a bitch like that from whoring around is to shoot her." Ralph made similar comments to his friend, Arthur Williams. He reiterated his fear that his wife had been having an affair, and if he found out she had been messing around on him he would have to "blow her away." Based on these threats, the prosecutor, Mr. Joe Moseley, felt he could now charge Ralph Davis with the first-degree murder of his wife, Susan Davis. A second-degree charge would have only required proof of an intentional killing. Murder in the first degree required proof of the additional element of cool and full reflection prior to the killing.

THE TRIAL

The trial began on March 14, 1989 in Boone County with Judge Gene Hamilton presiding. In order to convict Ralph Davis of first-degree murder, the prosecutor, Joe Moseley, had to prove Susan Davis was dead, her husband killed her, and he fully reflected on the murder before her death. If convicted of first-degree murder, there were only two available options: Ralph could serve life in prison without the possibility of parole, or he could be put to death by lethal injection. Mr. Moseley was worried about having enough evidence for the conviction of murder without a corpse, but he had other concerns as well. This was the first case in Missouri and one of the first cases throughout the U.S. in which a person might be convicted based on the relatively new technology of DNA fingerprinting (Fig. 1.18).

The first day of the trial was devoted almost entirely to circumstantial evidence surrounding Susan Davis' death. Since there was no body, the fact that Susan was missing had to be proven by circumstantial evidence. The prosecution accomplished this by having witnesses testify to occurrences which would be expected if Susan were still alive and then proving that none of those occurrences happened.

FIGURE 1.18 Boone County Courthouse. Ralph Davis' trial for killing his wife commenced on March 14, 1989.

In other words, the prosecution had to prove the alleged victim's normal pattern of life had stopped at the time of her disappearance.

Evidence in this case included testimony from Susan's friends and co-workers of her devotion to her children and her mother. Susan's mother testified that there had been no contact with her daughter between June 8, 1986 and the time of the trial, a period of almost three years. The prosecution presented official records showing that Susan Davis had not registered an automobile, committed a traffic violation, filed an income tax return, paid withholding tax, or received unemployment since 1986. Additionally, two co-workers identified the ring found in the search of Ralph's office as being Susan's from her first marriage and testified that they had never seen her without it.

After offering circumstantial evidence of Susan's death, the prosecution's next order of business was to prove Ralph's involvement in

CASE 1 — MURDER OF A WIFE

Susan's disappearance and any possible pre-planning of that disappearance.

The best evidence of Ralph's involvement was that he hid Susan's car and denied knowledge of its whereabouts until confronted with the rental agreement. Eyewitness testimony from the manager of Apache-U-Store-It and the taxi driver, coupled with the signed rental agreement and discarded bill from Apache found in Ralph's office, provided ample proof of his possession of Susan's car the day she was reported missing. Surprisingly, the Apache manager identified Ralph in court as the person who had rented the storage unit after failing to pick him out of a photographic lineup on the day the car was discovered. Also, in his statement to police the day he was arrested for murder, Ralph admitted he had possession of Susan's car and had later hidden it at the Apache-U-Store-It facility.

The evidence of the element of "cool and full reflection" on Ralph's part was not as strong. Normally, proof of planning is the best evidence of "reflection." Here, the statements made to Holste and Arthur Williams about "shooting" or "blowing away" Susan showed that he was at least considering killing his wife. The purchase of the shotgun just hours before Susan was last seen alive was presented to show some degree of pre-planning on Ralph's part.

Although evidence of motive is normally a necessity in convincing a jury of guilt beyond a reasonable doubt, it does not have to be proven. Susan Davis would have been the main witness to testify against Ralph if the criminal cases about his abuse had gone to trial. With Susan no longer available to testify, the criminal charges, which might have led to Davis' imprisonment, had to be dropped. Additionally, Ralph's desire for custody of the children and evidence of a substantial trust fund which he would control if his wife was out of the way were also presented as possible motives.

At this point in the trial, if the jury believed from the circumstantial evidence that Susan Davis was dead, there was ample evidence tying Ralph Davis to her death. The prosecution presented two days of expert scientific evidence to remove any doubt about Susan's death (Fig. 1.19).

In addition, prosecutors used a facsimile of the Ford Escort as background for all of the evidence found in the car. The prosecution wanted to impress the jury by bringing Susan's car into the courtroom. Since the car was too large to bring in its entirety and the police were reluctant to dismantle a critical piece of evidence, a reasonable alternative had to be found.

A local insurance company provided all but the engine compartment of an identical 1985 Ford Escort. The interior was removed and the remaining shell was cut into four sections. At the close of the second day of the trial, the shell was brought into the courtroom and reassembled. Over a period of almost eighteen hours, crime scene investigators installed the actual interior of Susan Davis' car into the

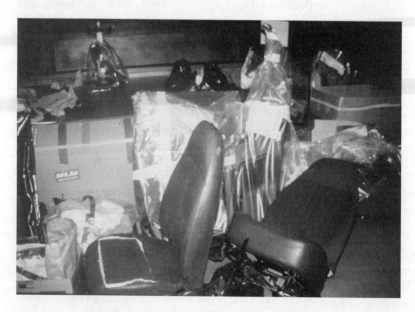

FIGURE 1.19 The entire inside of Susan's car was kept for evidence since her car was the crime scene.

borrowed shell. The shotgun pellets, bone fragments, head liner and visors with tissue remains, air fresheners, paper towels, cracked windshield, and doors with shattered glass were included (Figs. 1.20–1.24).

When the jury took their seats on the third morning of the trial, the car and all of its contents were visible directly in front of them. One of the investigators testified as to how the car had been dismantled and re-constructed, and the exhibit was then entered into evidence. At that point the judge permitted the jury to leave the jury box and inspect the car and its contents.

After the inspection, the defense requested that the car be removed from the courtroom. The prosecution pointed out to the judge that the

FIGURE 1.20 A Ford Escort similar to Susan's was used in the courtroom. It was stripped and modified for presentation to the jury.

FIGURE 1.21 The evidence from Susan's car was placed in the specially modified car.

FIGURE 1.22 The evidence technician took eighteen hours to make the car look like the original crime scene.

FIGURE 1.23 This is the completed car, including air fresheners (arrows), as seen from the jury box.

FIGURE 1.24 The car was kept intact under a tarp in order for it to be used by the prosecutor in his closing arguments.

car was going to be used in the closing argument, so it would have to be dismantled, reconstructed before summation, and then dismantled again. The prosecution argued that this eighteen-hour procedure was unnecessary since the car could be moved away from the jury and covered with a tarp. The court therefore denied the defense request, and for the remainder of the trial, the victim's car, hidden under a bright blue tarp in the courtroom, loomed over the defendant's shoulder.

All of the evidence found inside the car was introduced with little opposition from the defense. The defense team did attempt to discredit some of the opinions, but this was not the crux of their defense.

The forensic anthropologist, Dr. Stout, testified that the bone fragments found in the car came from the face of a person. However, he did admit there was a slight possibility that the fragments could also have come from the face of a cow. Many of the people involved in this case saw the humor in imagining a cow being shot in the front seat of a Ford Escort. Dr. Stout also discussed the presence of tetracycline in the bone and suggested that it had probably been present for less than two months in the victim's body. Susan Davis' prescriptions for tetracycline had been filled within two months prior to her disappearance.

Dr. Stout also explained that he sent the bone fragment with the gray smudge to another laboratory on the University of Missouri campus for analysis. The expert who performed the test testified that he used a scanning electron microscope to prove the presence of lead and antimony in the smudge. He also compared these findings to some of the pellets in the shells taken from Ralph's home and discovered the presence of similar elements.

The consulting forensic pathologist, Dr. Dix, also testified. It was his opinion that a homicide had occurred in the car. An injury to the face resulting in the amount of blood found in the car would not be a survivable injury. The defense had little rebuttal except to attempt to confuse the anthropologist's opinion regarding his 100% certainty that the bones were from a human and not a cow.

CASE 1 — MURDER OF A WIFE

The most important evidence in this case was the DNA. The prosecution was well aware that for a conviction to occur, they must prove the blood in the car belonged to Susan Davis. Before the trial, there was a *Frye* hearing on the merits of DNA fingerprinting. Prior to the admission of scientific evidence which had not yet received wide acceptance in courts of law, the evidence had to pass the *Frye* test, a standard set out in *Frye v. United States* (1923). The court ruled in this case that DNA evidence had gained general acceptance in the scientific community and Cellmark Laboratories had followed generally accepted procedures in this case.

The sole witness to testify at the *Frye* hearing was Dr. Daniel Garner, the Director of Laboratories for Cellmark Diagnostics. Dr. Garner testified that the scientific test at issue was generally known as DNA probe technology and had been in use since 1975 in the field of genetic disease. In the field of criminal detection, the same technique was given the name of DNA fingerprinting. He testified that this method of DNA analysis was considered to be reliable and accepted by the scientific community. He explained in great depth the procedures used in this method of testing. Finally, he presented the results of the testing in the Davis case. Judge Hamilton ruled that the DNA test procedure passed the *Frye* test and could be presented at trial based on the evidence from Cellmark. Therefore, the opinions of the expert from Cellmark Diagnostics could be heard by the jury during the trial.

Dr. Garner explained the laboratory findings to the jury. The samples tested included bloodstains from the car and blood from Ralph, Angela and Robbie Davis. Because each child received roughly half of his or her genetic material from the father and half from the mother, some of the matches in the testing should logically connect to the mother and some to the father. If there were no matches between the children and the stains from the car, then the blood in the car could not be Susan's.

Dr. Garner concluded to a reasonable degree of scientific certainty that the bloodstains in the car came from the mother of Robbie and Angela Davis. The DNA pattern of Angela Davis matched completely with that of Ralph Davis and the bloodstains from the car. There was no more than a 1 in 190,000 possibility that the bloodstains were not from the mother. The test result for Robbie Davis showed one line which deviated slightly from the result for the blood stain; although this deviation was within the limits of accuracy of the test, the witness chose to interpret it as a genetic mutation. Based upon this conservative assumption, Dr. Garner testified that the odds were 1 in 510 that anyone other than Robbie's mother was the source of the bloodstains. Combining the degrees of probability from the two children, Dr. Garner testified that the possibility that the blood in the car came from anyone other than the children's mother was 1 in 22,000,000 (almost four times the total world population) (Figs. 1.25–1.27).

Ralph Davis took the stand in his own defense. He recanted his most recent story that he had taken Susan's car away from her and that

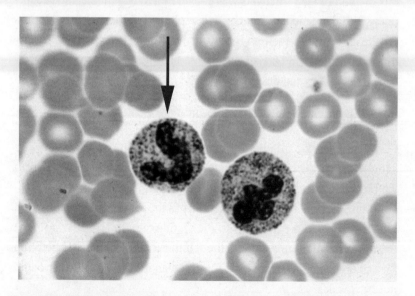

FIGURE 1.25 The blood in the car was analyzed for DNA. The nucleus (dark material inside this white cell) contains the DNA. The surrounding red blood cells do not contain DNA because they do not have a nucleus.

CASE 1 — MURDER OF A WIFE

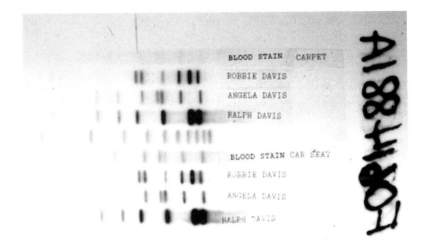

FIGURE 1.26 This is the DNA comparison study of Ralph, the children and the blood from the car.

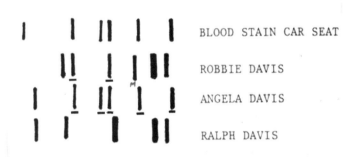

FIGURE 1.27 A simplified version of the DNA test was also shown to the jury. The underlined portions of DNA from the children were matches to either Ralph or the blood from the car. The one labeled with an 'm' was an acceptable mutation of one of the bands.

she had cut her hand by smashing it through the car window, but he admitted putting the vehicle into storage and forging her name on an insurance form. He said he had hired two men to take the Ford Escort from his wife, and that the blood and the broken window were present when the car was delivered to him. He had never given this account to the police and no evidence beyond his testimony was offered by the defense to support his latest version of events.

In its closing argument, the defense pointed out to the jury that without a body, they could never be sure that Susan Davis was really dead. The defense asked the jury to consider how they would feel if, some years later, Susan reappeared. The last question to the jury was how could they be certain beyond a reasonable doubt that Susan Davis was dead when no evidence of a body was presented

The prosecution answered that all that was left of Susan's body was in fact presented to the jury. The bone fragments, human tissue, and a large amount of blood found in the car were what remained of Susan after Ralph disposed of the rest of the body. Ralph had been smart enough to hide most of the body where it could never be found, but he inadvertently left enough of it to be positively identified through scientific testing and expert testimony. The prosecutor pointed out to the jury that they had two choices: reward Ralph Davis for being smart enough to hide Susan's body where it could not be found or punish him for cold-bloodedly murdering his wife, disposing of her body and lying to her children about her abandoning them. The final statement to the jury was a quote from a judge's opinion on the appeal in another murder case where no body had been found: "The fact that a defendant successfully disposes of the body of his murder victim does not entitle him to an acquittal. That is one form of success for which society has no reward."

After two hours of deliberation, the jury found Ralph Davis guilty as charged of first-degree murder. In the punishment phase, the state called three witnesses to testify about Ralph's physical abuse of Susan in an assault some three weeks before her disappearance, the resulting criminal charges, and the details of the trust fund. The defense presented the testimony of eight witnesses to convince the jury that Ralph should spend the remainder of his life in prison and not be put to death. The jury returned a sentence of death. The aggravating factors they found were that Ralph Davis murdered his wife for the purpose of using her money and trust fund and because she was the sole witness against him in two cases, one a pending prosecution for assault in the third degree and the other, a violation of a protection order.

Ralph Davis spent ten years appealing the court's decision. He was executed by lethal injection on April 28, 1999.

CASE 2

Murder of a Child

THE MISSING GIRL

Ramia Jere Montgomery, the daughter of Cathryn Williams, was a pretty, 5-year-old child. Intelligent and outspoken, she did not trust strangers. Both mother and daughter lived at 1017 Eletta Blvd. in Columbia, Missouri. Part of an extended family numbering more than twenty, including sisters and their children, they lived within blocks of each other in a Housing Authority Project. The entire family and friends had moved from East St. Louis, Illinois to Columbia in 1988.

On Saturday morning, November 11, 1989, Ramia went over to her aunt Bertha's house (1102 Eletta Blvd.) to play. Her mother saw her playing in Bertha's yard at 1:00 before she left for the store. When she returned at 4:00 p.m., she couldn't see Ramia in Bertha's yard, so Cathryn checked her house and yard and questioned a few neighbors about Ramia's whereabouts, but no one knew where she was. She did not see Ramia on Saturday evening or on Sunday, but she was not too concerned because it was normal for Ramia to spend the weekends at the home of one or more of her aunts and return on Monday mornings to attend school. But on Monday, November 13, Ramia did not return home before school. Cathryn called the school after checking the bus stop at 11:50 a.m., the usual time Ramia would catch the bus. She went home again, and after a brief but unsuccessful search, called the police. When Cathryn had last seen her, Ramia was wearing a green dress trimmed with white lace, white tights, and white shoes (Figs. 2.1 and 2.2),

Numerous friends, volunteers, and the police began a search for Ramia at 12:45 p.m. on Eletta Blvd. At 1:50 Sgt. Ken Smith and Detective Susan Stolz of the Columbia Police Department (CPD) interviewed Cathryn and were given a photograph of Ramia. Officer Smith requested help with the search, and a helicopter from the University of Missouri Hospitals and Clinics responded. The hospital helicopter had participated in air searches before and was glad to help until the highway patrol could furnish an aircraft.

Sgt. Jack Phillips of the CPD helped organize the ground search. Between 2:30 and 2:45 p.m., Sgt. Phillips was approached by Norman Wickizer, a boyfriend of one of Ramia's aunts. Wickizer asked if anyone had searched an area northeast of where the two men stood at the time. Phillips indicated to Wickizer that a team was checking the woods. In response, Wickizer suggested that a pond 200-300 yards to the northeast should be searched. Phillips replied that a helicopter was on the way to help search that area, and if Wickizer wanted to be helpful, he should join the volunteers who were searching a wooded area to the south (Figs. 2.3 and 2.4).

The hospital's helicopter arrived about 3:30 p.m. Sgt. Smith boarded the helicopter. Inside were the pilot, Syd Morrow, paramedic Ken Myers, and nurse Cheryl Tuggle. The pilot flew in a northeasterly direction and within ten minutes, Ken Myers spotted a body and pointed it out to Sgt. Smith. When Smith looked out the aircraft window, he first saw a man waving his arms and then he saw the body of a child. As the helicopter flew closer, the man waving his arms started pointing away from the body toward another area.

Within two minutes of discovering the man waving his arms and the child's body, the helicopter landed and Smith was on the ground. Knowing that his first obligation was to protect the scene until it could be processed by the crime scene technicians, Smith had to stop the

CASE 2 — MURDER OF A CHILD

FIGURE 2.1 Ramia Montgomery before her murder. (Courtesy of the Columbia Daily Tribune).

FIGURE 2.2 Ramia's mother, Cathryn Williams, is accompanied by a friend. (Courtesy of the Columbia Daily Tribune).

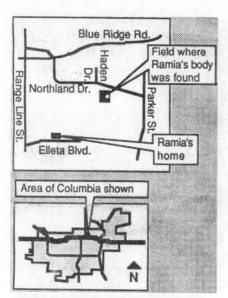

FIGURE 2.3 Ramia's neighborhood and where her body was discovered. (Courtesy of the Columbia Daily Tribune).

FIGURE 2.4 The crime scene was in the woods outlined by the arrows. Eletta Blvd. is in the lower left corner.

unknown arm waver from walking near the body. Nurse Tuggle checked the body while Smith secured the scene, but she found no signs of life. Sgt. Smith then began talking to Norman Wickizer, the man who had been waving at the helicopter (Figs. 2.5 and 2.6).

CASE 2 — MURDER OF A CHILD

FIGURE 2.5 Ramia's body was discovered in the grass next to a tree.

FIGURE 2.6 Once the body was removed, the tree was marked for ease of finding the location in the future.

During the ensuing discussion, Wickizer told Smith he was the dead girl's uncle and pointed to a nearby tree where he said he had found the girl's dress. He also stated he had taken his shirt and placed it on a branch so the tree would be easy to locate. Smith directed Wickizer to talk to Officer Susan Stoltz who had now arrived on the scene. As he met Officer Stoltz, Wickizer put his cigarette out in the grass.

Smith left Wickizer and Stolz and walked in the direction of the marked tree. He readily found the tree with a plaid shirt hanging on one of its branches. He circled the tree, but didn't see any other clothing. After separating many of the branches and peering inside, he discovered a ball-shaped wad of clothing. The ball of clothing was approximately three feet off the ground, near the trunk, and was later measured to be 45 inches from the outside of the branches.

A perimeter was set up around the body with yellow line tape. Officer David Nelson of the CPD began to photograph the crime scene. Ramia's body was lying face down in the weeds near a tree. She was naked and there were obvious signs of foul play with blood on her back and rectal areas. Nelson completed his photographs and the medical examiner, Dr. Ed Adelstein arrived on the scene. Dr. Adelstein briefly examined the body and then directed its removal to the medical examiner's office.

Officer Nelson also photographed the tree that contained the ball of clothing. He said that, like Sgt. Smith, he couldn't see the clothing until he pulled down several branches. Nelson removed the wad of clothing and examined it. Within the square bundle were a green dress, torn white cotton tights, and the shoes her mother had described as the apparel she last saw her daughter wearing. The sleeves of the dress were tied in a knot around the rest of the articles. Sticks and seedpods were clinging to the dress. A piece of the dress was torn away and this torn portion was included in the bundle. Officer Nelson also collected a Marlboro cigarette butt from the ground adjacent to the tree (Figs. 2.7–2.9).

CASE 2 — MURDER OF A CHILD

FIGURE 2.7 The tree containing Ramia's clothing. Wickizer placed his shirt on the tree to mark where he had found Ramia's clothing.

FIGURE 2.8 A police officer is holding down the branches to view the bundle of Ramia's clothing deep within the tree.

FIGURE 2.9 The bundle of Ramia's clothing found in the tree included her dress with a torn portion, part of her tights, and her shoes.

Over the next few hours and during the next day, a wider area of the crime scene was searched. Investigators discovered that the location of the body was not the only assault site. The girl's panties were discovered in one location and a portion of her tights in another. Blood was discovered on the ground near another tree. An Oh Henry candy bar wrapper and a Bic lighter were also discovered and collected as evidence (Figs. 2.10–2.12).

FIGURE 2.10 An Oh Henry candy bar wrapper found at the scene had similar lot numbers to some of the candy bars in Norman's home.

FIGURE 2.11 Panties discovered in the woods were thought to be Ramia's; however, her mother would never admit they belonged to Ramia.

CASE 2 — MURDER OF A CHILD

FIGURE 2.12 A part of Ramia's tights was found in the woods (above). These were later matched to a portion of the tights found in the tree. The state crime lab was able to match the main portion of Ramia's tights found in the tree with the torn portion discovered in the grass (below).

THE AUTOPSY

Dr. Ed Adelstein, Medical Examiner of Boone County, performed the autopsy at 8:00 p.m. on the same day the body was discovered. He found numerous fresh linear scratches on Ramia's left upper arm and old scratches on the ankles and forearms. The only bruise on her body was a recently developed one on the back of her neck. There was dried blood on her back, inner left thigh, left little finger, and face. Foam was in her nose and there was a part of a maple leaf in her mouth. Teeth marks were noticeable on the inside of her cheek.

The most significant external injuries were in the vaginal and rectal areas. There were obvious signs of rape and sodomy with tearing and abrasions of the labia, vagina, and rectum. Vaginal, oral, and anal swabs were taken and sent to the state crime lab for analysis (Figs. 2.13–2.15.)

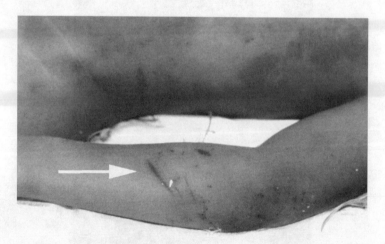

FIGURE 2.13 There were scratches (abrasions) on Ramia's arms and chest in addition to the neck and vaginal injuries.

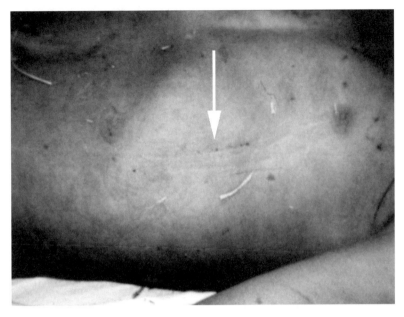

FIGURE 2.14 Abrasions on Ramia's chest.

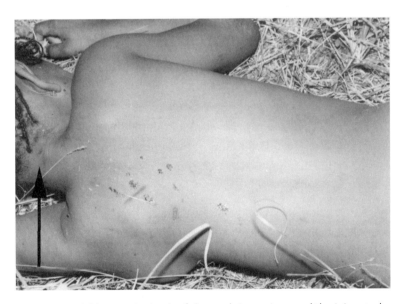

FIGURE 2.15 A blow to the back of the neck (arrow) caused the injury to her spinal cord.

Internally, the injuries were impressive in the pelvic and neck regions. There was abundant blood from the rectal and vaginal tears. A dissection of the neck revealed marked hemorrhage around the spinal cord, but x-rays and direct visualization revealed no fractures of the neck bones. Microscopic examination of the spinal cord failed to show any direct damage to the spinal cord.

Dr. Adelstein concluded that Ramia died as the result of spinal cord injury from a blow to the back of her neck. It was his opinion that this injury impaired her breathing. He also believed the bleeding from the injuries to her rectal/vaginal areas were contributing factors in her death.

THE INVESTIGATION

Interviews with Norman Wickizer

Shortly after Ramia's body was discovered, Officer Stolz escorted Wickizer to the police station for an interview. When questioned about the clothing, Wickizer told Officer Stoltz he noticed Ramia's dress when he was standing near the tree. He made no mention of having to move branches or look into the tree to locate the clothing. Wickizer then drew a sketch for Stoltz indicating what he did regarding the search. After briefly looking at the sketch, Stolz left the room and when she returned she saw the sketch crumpled up in a ball on the table. She thought this strange; however, she didn't ask why he wadded up the diagram and Wickizer didn't explain. He was allowed to leave.

Later that night, Wickizer was interviewed again by Officer Nelson and Detective Randy McMillin. Wickizer told Detective McMillin about the events of the day when Ramia was last seen. He said that earlier in the day, Ramia came walking into his house at approximately 12:30 p.m. She was hungry so he fixed her a couple of hot dogs, but after that, he didn't see her again.

Wickizer gave more details of his actions earlier in the day to Officer Nelson. During the search, he was walking toward the cedar tree which contained the clothing when the light green color of Ramia's dress caught his eye. He also stated he was specifically looking for Ramia's dress because he knew that if something had happened to her she might not have her dress on. He also left the men with whom he was searching, including Homer Collins, for about ten to fifteen minutes before he discovered the dress. The location of the tree with the clothing was approximately one-quarter mile from Eletta Blvd.

When challenged about the discovery of the dress by Officer Nelson, Wickizer changed his story. He stated that he was walking so close to the tree that it brushed his arm and then he glanced to his side and spotted the clothing. He also said he was the last person to see Ramia in that dress.

Wickizer told Officer Nelson that he smoked a cigarette after he found Ramia's clothing in the tree while waiting for the helicopter, but carried the cigarette up to the rear of the house at 2801 North Lynn Drive. When asked if it was possible that the cigarette butt found near the tree in which the clothing was discovered was his, he admitted it was a possibility because he often smoked in the woods and it was possible he dropped a cigarette nearby. He also said his fingerprints might be on Ramia's body because he touched her when she was in his house eating lunch. Nelson asked Wickizer to identify the Bic lighter found in the woods, and he agreed that it looked like the ones he used. He added that it could be his because he had lost lighters like that in the woods.

Wickizer's statements concerning the clothing didn't ring true to the detectives, so they considered him a suspect from the beginning of the investigation. The detectives requested hair, blood, and saliva samples, and Wickizer agreed to supply samples. Officer Ralph Ross took pubic hair combings and removed pubic hair and head hair samples from Norman on November 13. At approximately 11:00 p.m. the same night, Wickizer was taken to the University Medical Center with Detective Ward where E.R. nurse Penny Baugh took a blood sample which she placed into a container brought by Officer Ross. Nurse Baugh also obtained blood and saliva samples and placed them onto a card for analysis.

Leads

Shortly after the discovery of the body, the Major Case Squad assembled. A Major Case Squad is composed of members from surrounding law enforcement jurisdictions. This team is activated when there is a homicide investigation that might stretch the resources of the jurisdiction in which the crime occurred. Usually the squad spends a few days to a few weeks running down leads to find the assailant, providing much needed extra manpower for a short period of time. The squad's work prevents disruption of the day-to-day work of the requesting agency. The requesting county reimburses the other agencies sending the help. All members of the squad have received special training in order to contribute to the investigation. In this case, members came from other towns within Boone County as well as from seven other counties.

Capt. Veach, Watch Commander for the Columbia Police Dept., commanded the members of the Mid-Missouri Major Case Squad. He assembled the squad at 8:00 a.m. on Tuesday, November 14. Each day, approximately fifteen officers gathered to help the CPD follow leads in the investigation. There were 45 leads and 36 contacts made within a few days (Fig. 2.16).

Homer Collins, a security officer for the Housing Authority, told officers he had received a phone call at his repair shop, Collin's Auto Repair, telling him that Ramia was missing and his help was needed in the search. Paul Modesitt, a customer and friend of Homer's, was in the shop at the time. Homer asked Paul if he would like to come along to help look for a missing girl. Paul agreed, and the two men drove to the first parking lot along Eletta Blvd. There they saw Nor-

FIGURE 2.16 Law enforcement from seven other counties helped the Columbia Police Department in following leads.

man Wickizer, who joined the two men in their search of an area north of Eletta. They spread out and Norman disappeared from view. Homer and Paul then saw the helicopter and assumed the child had been found, so they discontinued their search. According to Homer, the only occurrence worthy of note was a remark made by Norman while the three of them were in the truck on the way to search the woods. Wickizer told the other two that it would be hard to find a dead, naked black child. Modesitt thought the statement strange because it sounded as if Wickizer knew the child's body would be discovered unclothed.

Cathryn Williams was interviewed again after her daughter's body was discovered. She said that Ramia and four other children had eaten lunch at her sister Bertha's house on Saturday. The lunch consisted of bologna, cheese, and juice. This contradicted Norman's statements that he had fixed Ramia two hot dogs the same day. Cathryn also said Ramia was happy on Friday because her grandmother, Glover Williams, had made her a new green dress. This is the same dress she was wearing on the Saturday when she was last seen.

Cathryn told investigators that when she could not find Ramia, she thought it possible that her brother, James McDaniel, from East St. Louis, may have taken Ramia back to visit her grandmother who also lived in East St. Louis. Ramia had lived with this grandmother from the age of two months until she started school just two months earlier. She called the police after scouring the neighborhood and calling Ramia's school. The assistant principal had told Cathryn that her daughter was not in school, and so she had returned home, searched again, and then called the police at approximately 12:30 p.m.

The police also interviewed Christine Dampier, Cathryn's sister and Norman Wickizer's girlfriend. She said she stayed home most of Saturday. She left to go shopping before 1 p.m. and sometime prior to her leaving, Norman had been picked up by Tony, a man who also worked for the Housing Authority. They went to clean out a shed, and returned with some barrels they placed behind the house. Then they left again. Christine said she last saw Ramia around noon playing in a yard down the street. She came home after shopping and remained there until 6:30 when she left to go to church. Christine knew Norman had gone fishing with David and Mark Neely during the afternoon. She didn't arrive home from church until approximately 10:45 p.m. and Bertha had already picked up her children. The next day she attended church in Brunswick from 9:00 a.m. to 9:00 p.m. and didn't realize Ramia was missing until she was called at the Food Bank Monday morning. Her work schedule was usually 9:00 a.m.–12:30 p.m.

Bertha McDaniel was also interviewed by investigators. She stated that she arrived at Q.T. Grayson's home at 1302 Eletta to give her a Jeri Curl perm at approximately 12:30 p.m. and she was accompanied by Ramia and two other children. The children watched television for approximately 45 minutes and were sent outside to play. All of them remained at Grayson's house until 4:20 p.m. When Bertha departed, she was carrying a child and could not take the hair supplies with her. Grayson then gave Ramia and the other two children playing in the yard some of the supplies and told them to take them to Bertha's house. They did so and ten minutes later were back playing in Grayson's yard.

Grayson's daughter, Dorothy (Dot) also saw the children playing in the yard at about 4:30. Dot advised the children to go home because it was getting dark. However, as Dot later told her mother, the children didn't go home, but headed in the direction of the park. This was the last time either of the two women saw Ramia.

When Ms. Grayson was asked about who might have murdered Ramia, she said, "I'm not saying." She did say the person who did it was "right under everybody's nose," but she didn't think Wickizer did it. When asked if Sylvester, the boyfriend of Ramia's mother, could have done it, she responded, "I don't know." She said only that everyone should pray and the truth would come out.

Nekima Brownlee, the ten-year-old daughter of Bertha McDaniel, was one of the two children playing with Ramia at Ms. Grayson's house when they were sent home by Dot Grayson. She stated it was "half-way nighttime" when she suggested they go home. Nekima, her cousin Treveon, and Ramia were throwing rocks in the air when she was advised to go home. Nekima started up the hill and then began running, but the door to her home at 1102 Eletta was locked. Nekima looked back down the street, didn't see Ramia, and then went to Christine's house at 1210 Eletta. She knew Treveon had gone home; however, she didn't know Ramia's whereabouts.

After Nekima went into Christine's house, she watched *Wheel of Fortune* at 6:30, and then *227*. She stated that Ramia came in later and went into another room with Miesha, Bertha's daughter. Norman was also there at the time and took a television into his bedroom to watch. She stated that there was no one else in the room with him. Nekima remained at the house until 10:45 p.m. when her mother picked her up.

Nekima was the only person who said Ramia was present that evening. None of the other children remembered Ramia being there.

Bertha McDaniel told investigators that she normally "keeps" Christine's house on weekends, but did not follow her regular schedule that weekend because she wanted to attend church. She left her home at approximately 7:00 p.m. because church began at 7:30 in Jefferson City (30 miles away). Before leaving for church, Bertha dropped off her four children at Christine's home, and picked up Christine's three other friends. Norman and Miesha, her daughter, stayed to look after the four kids. Bertha returned around 10:45 p.m. and picked up three of her children and one of Cathryn's daughters. Someone had told her that her son had already gone home and she assumed Ramia had returned to her mother's home.

Investigators also questioned Pearlie Moore who lived near Eletta Blvd. She saw Ramia on Eletta the afternoon of November 11, between 1:30 and 1:45 p.m. Pearlie stated that Ramia considered Wickizer her uncle and assumed their relationship was "fine." The same afternoon, Moore saw Wickizer between 1:45 and 2:00 walking up the hill on Eletta, appearing to be headed home. Norma had been speaking to Mark Nealy, who lived with Pearlie, and Eddy Fulton, another friend. Moore said Wickizer was wearing a gold-colored jumpsuit. Later that afternoon she again saw Wickizer while looking out her kitchen window at a little past 4:00. She remembered because she had looked at the clock on the microwave. Pearlie saw Wickizer wiping his knife on the grass, but didn't think this very unusual since he routinely killed snakes with a knife. He was wearing blue jeans and a gray t-shirt.

David Nealy, Mark's brother, lived with Pearlie Moore on Eletta. He stated he was with Wickizer from 10:30 a.m. to 2:00 p.m. on the Saturday Ramia was last seen. At about 2:00 p.m., Wickizer, David Nealy and his brother decided to go fishing. Wickizer said he had to go home and left. He asked them to meet him at his house in 10-15 minutes. At that time he was wearing a jumpsuit. After thirty minutes, the two brothers went to pick up Wickizer at his house, but he wasn't there. The brothers asked Wickizer's girlfriend, Christine, about Norman's whereabouts. She said he was somewhere out in the woods. The Nealy brothers waited for Wickizer who finally arrived back at the parking lot in front of their house at approximately 4:30 p.m. They said they first saw him coming out of the woods. He was wearing jeans and a shirt, not his jumpsuit, and his clothes were covered with "sticker bugs." They all went fishing then at Little Dixie Lake.

On the way to Little Dixie Lake, the Nealys questioned Wickizer about what he was doing in the woods, but Wickizer didn't say much. The brothers thought their friend was acting strangely. When they arrived at the lake to fish, Norman didn't fish. Instead, he spent the entire time picking the stickers off his clothing. The brothers later corroborated each other's statements.

Pearlie Moore saw Wickizer the next day, November 12, at approximately 10:30 or 11:00 a.m. in the front yard. He was speaking to Mark Nealy before he left with Mark to go over to David's house.

Mark Nealy said that Wickizer came to his house on November 12 to see if he wanted to go fishing at Finger Lakes. They walked to David Nealy's house and asked him to go along. While waiting for David Nealy, Mark questioned Wickizer about why he took so long in the woods the day before and wasted all their good fishing time. At first Wickizer refused to answer, but when coaxed, he replied, "Man, you know, I found me a good place out there in the woods where you can go tear up some pussy." He also stated, "Man, I had me some good tight pussy out there in the woods yesterday." A little later he remarked to Mark again that he had some "tight stuff" in the woods the day before. He never mentioned looking for worms which was what he had told the police.

David and Mark Neely were very good friends of Norman's, but they both admitted they believed he killed Ramia. They said that Norman had pointed out young girls before and said that he wanted to have sex with them. Mark also remembered Norman saying he had a "fuck place" in the woods.

Later, the Nealy brothers looked at photographs of Ramia's clothing. They said the sticker bugs on her clothing appeared to be the same as those they had seen on Wickizer's clothing when he emerged from the woods.

On November 14, Bobbie Carter, a Columbia resident who did not live near the area of the murder, was sitting outside the old Wabash train depot reading the newspaper account of Ramia's death. While reading, a white male had walked up, observed her reading the newspaper, and mentioned that it was really terrible what had happened to the little girl. She said the man also stated that he had taken part in the search the day before and that the girl had been raped and sodomized. Carter then commented that the little girl's teeth had been knocked out and she had scratches on her face according to the article, but that it did not mention that the girl had been raped and sodomized. The man replied that the little girl died from a blow to the back of her head. Carter later realized this information was also not included in the news article. The man disappeared and she didn't know where he went after their conversation. She described the man as being in his early 30's, having near-shoulder length, oily, dark hair, a moustache that covered the top of his lip, and a medium build. He may have been 5'9"-10" in height. The description matched that of Norman Wickizer. Later, Ms. Carter was shown photographs of Wickizer and others. She was unable to positively identify the man who had spoken to her at the bus stop.

Wickizer quickly became a suspect because of the inconsistencies in his story and the statements he had made to his friends. A search warrant was issued for his residence at 1210 Eletta Blvd. Oh Henry candy bars and wrappers were collected from the living room, kitchen, master bedroom and other bedrooms. The lot numbers on the candy bar wrappers collected at his residence matched the lot numbers of the Oh Henry wrapper discovered in the woods (Fig. 2.17).

In the interview just prior to his arrest, Norman said he had a "fixation on masturbation," which he would do alone or in front of his

CASE 2 — MURDER OF A CHILD 53

FIGURE 2.17 Oh Henry candy bars were discovered at the Wickizer's residence in the kitchen, an ashtray (left), and in a jar adjacent to the bed (right).

girlfriend. He admitted he masturbated many times in the woods and even did it in the woods on both November 11 and 12. After being pressed many times about killing the child, he kept saying, "I didn't hurt the little girl."

The police wanted to have Norman's knife analyzed for the presence of Ramia's blood. On December 15, they found him standing in his yard, and when asked for the knife, he told the police to enter the house and ask Christine for it. Christine retrieved the knife from the bedroom and gave it to the police; however, eventual examination of the knife failed to reveal the presence of blood.

The same afternoon the knife was recovered, the DNA tests of Wickizer's blood from Cellmark Diagnostic arrived. These results implicated Wickizer. The police now had enough evidence for an arrest. They went to Wickizer's residence and arrested him at approximately 5:30 p.m. The next day, a media conference at the CPD confirmed that Wickizer had been arrested for the murder of Ramia Montgomery (Figs. 2.18 and 2.19).

CASE 2 — MURDER OF A CHILD

FIGURE 2.18 Norman Wickizer at work explaining his innocence to the press. (Courtesy of the Columbia Daily Tribune).

FIGURE 2.19 Norman Wickizer's arrest photo.

WICKIZER'S BACKGROUND

Past Criminal History

In 1971, Wickizer was committed for a year to a juvenile detention center in Indianapolis for delinquency. According to his parents, he was incorrigible, stole $20 from a relative and was habitually truant from school. In 1974, he was sentenced to the Indiana Youth Center in Plainfield, Indiana for second-degree burglary. He stole approximately $2600 worth of goods and a boat from a cottage along a river near his home in LaPorte County.

The following year, 1975, he was charged with three burglaries, but probably committed over one hundred. In 1976, he was arrested for possession of a controlled substance (marijuana), fined $100, and served 90 days in the Indiana State Penal Farm. A marijuana arrest occurred in 1979 and the same year he was arrested for the possession of a sawed-off shotgun. From 1981–85, Wickizer was incarcerated in Terre Haute, Indiana, and Hillsboro, Illinois for stealing. He next spent two and a half years in Minard Prison, Illinois for car theft.

Recent History

Prior to coming to Columbia, Wickizer lived in East St. Louis with Glover Williams, Ramia's grandmother. He had previously lived with a woman named Pamela for a year. Pamela had been the girlfriend of David Bell, a fellow inmate at Minard State Penitentiary. David asked Norman to take care of Pamela while he was in prison and sent him $1000 a month to do so. The money stopped coming to Norman when David died by hanging in prison. Norman said it was a homicide.

He moved to Columbia in 1988 and lived with Christine Dampier on Eletta Blvd. Norman started working for the Housing Authority on July 11, 1989 as a maintenance worker. He was still a Housing Authority employee when Ramia was murdered.

There were three to four allegations in Norman's file about sexual abuse in the months prior to Ramia's disappearance. One involved Wickizer and Shanika Cain.

Sharon Cain, mother of Shanika, an elementary school student, told the police she knew of two occasions when Norman touched Shanika inappropriately. The first was when he grabbed her child and swung her around in the air. The little girl was upset because he had touched her private parts. The other incident occurred when the child was spending the night at her grandmother's house. Shanika said Norman touched her while she was sleeping. When confronted with this, Norman said he was only pulling the covers over her and that was all. Sharon said she never trusted Norman after that and did not allow her daughter to spend nights at Christine's house.

Shanika was interviewed on November 16 at Blue Ridge Elementary School in the presence of Principal Dave Brunda. Shanika and Ramia were very good friends. When asked if she liked Norman, Shanika became visibly upset, shook her head negatively and teared up. When asked again, she shook her head and said, "No". When asked why, she said Norman tried to "get her once." He tried to touch her private parts, indicating her bottom, and he tried to grab her from behind. She said Norman tried to grab Latrisha once but Latrisha fought him off. Shanika waved her fists in the air to indicate what Latrisha had done. When another attempt was made to ask about Norman, Shanika became upset, started crying, stood up, and backed away. She was then asked if she wanted to talk to the counselor, Teresa Farugia. She indicated yes, the counselor was called to the room, and Shanika left with her.

There were many unsubstantiated rumors about Norman, including one involving the rape of a girl who had lived in the area and had since moved away. Another was that he had "messed" with his stepdaughters and had been mean to children. Norman had rubbed the young girls while making it look accidental, and had been in trouble before in Kentucky "for rape or some sort of sex charge." Janis Dampi-

CASE 2 — MURDER OF A CHILD

er told the police she thought Norman committed the murder. She believed her mother knew more about Norman than anyone else but was afraid to say anything because she was afraid of Norman's reaction if she spoke out.

Some members of the family told police that Norman had felt one young family member's breast after he had put four quarters down the front of her shirt. He was known to come up behind girls and grab them around the front, holding them tightly. One of the aunts did not want her children alone with Norman because of his inappropriate actions.

Dead End Leads

Police were told that Treveon Williams, the son of Kathy Williams, 1208 Eletta, had been playing with Ramia near dark on the day she was last seen. He was playing on the merry-go-round and she was sitting on the swing set. Then he didn't see her and went looking for her. Near the basketball court he saw a black man in a brown jumpsuit carrying Ramia off into the woods, trying to stuff her into an Army bag. He stated that he followed them into the woods and saw the man go into a white house, and there was another man in this house.

On November 16, Officer Stolz interviewed Traveon Williams. Kathy Williams had told Officer Susan Wooderson earlier that Traveon had reported he saw Ramia taken from the playground by a tall, black man. Officer Stolz took Traveon back to the playground to check out the story. Accompanying them was Traveon's stepfather, Anthony McKire.

Officer Stolz sat with Traveon in the playground area and asked him if he remembered the day Ramia was last seen. Traveon said he did and told Officer Stolz that he, Ramia, and Nekima had been playing on the swings and slide. Ramia played on the swings and did not come over to play on the slide with Nekima and him. When he looked up he saw a man standing near the basketball court. Traveon had told

Officer Wooderson earlier that a man had taken Ramia. At this point Officer Stolz, Mr. McKire, and Traveon walked over to the edge of the court.

Traveon said the man took Ramia into the woods. Officer Stolz asked Traveon to lead them in the direction the man traveled. The three of them began walking in the woods, and it soon became obvious that Traveon didn't know where he was or what direction they were traveling. The three eventually circled around back to the houses. After they finished walking in the woods, Officer Stolz asked Traveon if he was telling the truth about being in the woods that last Saturday. She told him the story about the little boy crying wolf and how important it was to tell the truth. After the story Traveon admitted he hadn't been out in the woods the day Ramia disappeared.

Officer Stolz gave Mr. Mckire a ride back to a Phillips 66 gas station after dropping off Traveon. While in the car, Mr. Mckire began pulling the stickers off his clothing. He said that he had seen Traveon shortly after dark the day Ramia disappeared and he didn't have any stickers on his clothing. Both agreed that it was unlikely Traveon had been in the woods the day Ramia disappeared.

Crime stoppers called on November 14 and said a girl in Ramia's class, Yvette, had seen the victim climb out of a window with a man chasing her. She told her mother that she saw the man kill the little girl. The follow-up revealed the little girl didn't live in the area, didn't really know Ramia, and had made up the story.

Officer Wooderson of the CPD called the Illinois State Police on November 17 and asked if anything similar to Ramia's case had occurred in the East St. Louis area. Agent Robyn Blanda said that in an area called Parksidel in Centerville, Illinois, a homicide occurred involving a 6-year-old boy named Aree Hunt on July 13, 1989. The boy had a birthday party that day and later in the evening, he and another friend were approached by a heavyset black man who asked them if they wanted to make any money. Aree went with the man and his naked body was discovered the next day on an embankment near a canal. He had been beaten around the face and the semen in his rectum indicated he had been sexually molested. The assailant had not been found at the time of Ramia's murder.

The only other unsolved crime at the time in East St. Louis was the murder of a 16-year-old girl. She lived within a block of Aree Hunt and was beaten, raped and murdered on October 3, 1989 between 4:00 and 4:30 p.m. 40 yards from the bus stop on her way home after school, she was robbed of a watch, chain and $65 and was vaginally assaulted with a stick found nearby. These crimes were not thought to be connected with the death of Ramia (Figs. 2.20 and 2.21).

In Loving Memory Of

Ramia J. Montgomery
1984-1989

FIGURE 2.20 This is Ramia's funeral announcement.

FIGURE 2.21 At least 125 people attended the funeral. (Photo courtesy of the Columbia Daily Tribune.)

Other Suspects

M.O., a 19-year-old from Nigeria, was stopped while he was jogging east on Eletta Blvd. on November 15. The police picked him up because previously he had been caught peeping in windows at 1308 Eletta. He lived in Columbia with his father, had no job, and planned to study agriculture. He was being treated by a psychiatrist at the time, and not only consented to a mugshot, but also gave blood, hair, and fingerprint samples.

R.J., an ex-boyfriend of Janice Dampier, was reported to be "violent and goes off for no reason and breaks things." He had served time for abuse and was in the area at the time of Ramia's disappearance. The police contacted him and he agreed to furnish samples of blood, hair, and saliva for testing.

Frank White, of 113A Eletta, was reported to have frequented the woods. He lived in a trailer near the area. White grew up with his family in East St. Louis and knew Norman while in prison in Chester, Illinois. Norman was incarcerated for burglaries and White was serving time for manslaughter. He said the person who killed Ramia should be killed. According to White, Norman acted kind of crazy at times like pulling out a knife and waving it around. When asked about what would happen to a person in prison who had killed and sodomized a little girl, he said the assailant would be beaten and sexually victimized. White admitted he had taken part in such beatings, but he had never had sex with another man. He consented to giving blood, fingerprint, hair and saliva samples, and to having a photograph taken.

W.D. had been seen in the area around the time of the murder. He stated he had recently driven into Columbia with a load of watermelons to sell and had spoken to the lady in the first housing unit, but couldn't remember her name. W.D. and a friend had left Columbia to go hunting around noon on November 10 in Princeton, Missouri, and didn't return until around 7:00 p.m. two days later. He said he stayed at a friend's home in Princeton, but knew him only as Kevin. He agreed to have pubic hair, blood, and saliva collected for testing.

Lab Tests

DNA testing was performed on a semen stain found on Ramia's dress and blood from all the suspects, including Wickizer. Two specimens from Wickizer were tested, one from December 27, 1989 and the other from January 25, 1990. The tests were conducted by Cellmark Diagnostics in Germantown, Maryland. The December test patterns of the semen stains were similar to DNA samples obtained from Wickizer; however, they did not constitute a match according to Cellmark's standards. The January test patterns of Ramia's dress stains matched DNA samples obtained from Wickizer and the frequency of the banding pattern was 1 in 6500 (Fig. 2.22).

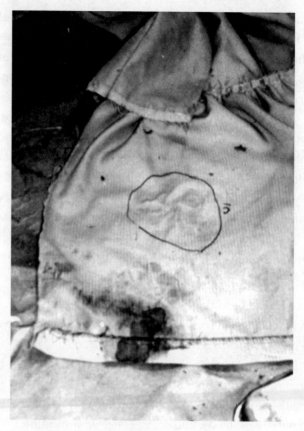

FIGURE 2.22 A semen stain was discovered on Ramia's dress (circled area). It was consistent with Wickizer's blood type.

Pubic hairs recovered from Ramia's dress were proven similar to known samples obtained from Wickizer. In addition, the semen collected from Ramia's dress revealed the presence of blood group substance H and the enzyme PGM type 2-1. This was consistent with the samples obtained from Wickizer, although approximately 13% of the general male population of the U.S. possesses both blood group substance H and PGM 2-1 in their semen. Finally, saliva containing blood group substance H was detected on the Marlboro cigarette butt found where Ramia's dress was discovered. The detection of blood group substance H is consistent with the saliva sample taken from Wickizer.

The DNA testing eliminated all other suspects.

THE TRIAL

In exchange for a waiver of the death penalty, on January 9, 1991, the defendant waived his right to trial by jury and a *Frye* hearing to challenge the admissibility of the DNA evidence. The prosecution's agreement to not seek the death penalty was based on two concerns: a jury's difficulty in assessing the complex and less than overwhelming DNA evidence and the medical examiner's opinion that the death could have been caused accidentally during the course of the sexual assaults. An accidental death under these circumstances would support a guilty finding of second-degree murder under the felony murder rule, but a conviction for the charged offense, murder in the first degree, would require a finding that the killing was done intentionally after cool and full reflection.

The prosecution believed that an experienced judge would be better able than twelve jurors to sort out conflicting testimony, weigh the strength of evidence and ignore red herrings raised by the defense. It was also believed that a judge was more likely than a jury to impose the maximum punishment of life imprisonment (with parole a possibility) if the defendant was found guilty of second-degree murder. A three-day bench trial commenced on February 26, 1991 with Judge Gene Hamilton presiding.

The prosecution opened the case by presenting testimony concerning the whereabouts of Ramia Montgomery on Saturday, November 11, 1989. The evidence was clearly established that Ramia was seen numerous times by many people on that day. Several neighbors and relatives, including Nekima Brownlee, thought that they had seen Ramia during the late afternoon and early evening of Saturday. However, under oath, many of these witnesses presented conflicting testimony. All of this confusion concerning Ramia's whereabouts during the time period when the Nealy brothers were waiting for Wickizer to go fishing created doubts in the minds of the jurors.

Next, the state offered photographic and testimonial evidence relating to the discovery of the body. Included in this evidence was the suspicious activity of the defendant, such as his suggestion that the police search an area very close to where the body was found and his preceding to the northeast when the police directed him to search south of the housing area. Also included was Wickizer's statement expressed prior to the discovery, of the difficulty in finding a little dead, naked black girl and his locating the well-hidden clothing with a cursory glance. There was also physical evidence (candy bar wrappers, a cigarette butt and Bic lighter) which connected the defendant to the scene and testimony relating to his statement that his fingerprints could quite possibly be found on the victim since he had touched her on Saturday (Figs. 2.23 and 2.24).

The morning of the second day of trial was devoted to testimony about Norman Wickizer's whereabouts on Saturday, November 11 and statements that he made that day and the next. Three witnesses, Pearlie Moore and the Nealy brothers, testified that the defendant was with them until approximately 2:00 p.m. when he returned to his house to prepare to go fishing. At that time, he was wearing a gold-colored jumpsuit. The defendant asked David and Mark Nealy to meet him at his home at about 2:30, but when they arrived, Christine Dampier, Wickizer's girlfriend, told them that he had gone somewhere out in the woods. He was next seen at 4:30 p.m. emerging from the woods and wearing blue jeans and a gray t-shirt. His clothing was covered with what the Nealy brothers described as "sticker bugs," similar to the ones found on Ramia's tights.

When the Nealy brothers asked the defendant what he had been doing in the woods, he responded that he had found a "fuck shop" and

CASE 2 — MURDER OF A CHILD

FIGURE 2.23 Aerial photos were used to mark the location of the evidence because the crime scene encompassed such a large area.

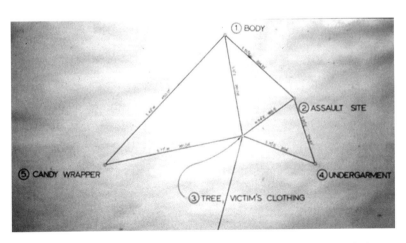

FIGURE 2.24 This diagram was used in conjunction with the aerial photographs to help explain the evidence to the jury.

some "tight stuff" or "tight pussy". He made similar statements to both brothers the following day, Sunday, November 12. Both witnesses testified that when the three of them left to go fishing, Wickizer seemed preoccupied and, at one point, looked scared. During the entire time they were at the lake, the defendant removed the "sticker bugs" from his clothing and did not participate in the fishing. David Nealy also testified that on the way to the lake, Wickizer was eating an Oh Henry candy bar.

The state's case concluded with testimony from expert witnesses concerning physical evidence found at the scene. Laboratory experts testified to the significance of the similarities between the pubic hairs recovered from Ramia and semen stains from her dress and the defendant's pubic hair and blood. None of these could be matched positively to Wickizer, although the comparisons were consistent with only 13 percent of the male population. Even the cigarette butt discovered near the clothing was consistent with his blood type.

A more specific link to the defendant was presented through testimony from Cellmark Laboratories personnel concerning their DNA testing in this case. Cellmark conducted two separate tests, almost one month apart, on evidence collected by Columbia Police. The testimony was that the first test was inconclusive but the second test indicated a match between the semen found on the victim's dress and blood samples taken from the defendant. The frequency of the banding pattern in the match was 1 in 6,500. This meant that for every 6,500 white males in the world population, a single man would have this specific banding pattern in his DNA This meant that only nine men in Boone County (the location of the crime) would have DNA that contained this pattern (Fig. 2.25).

In their case, the defense attempted to establish an alibi. A former Columbia police detective, Jim Arnold, testified that shortly after dark on the evening of November 11, he was walking his dog in a park approximately one mile from the location where Ramia's body was found. He testified that he heard a sound that he thought was a young

CASE 2 — MURDER OF A CHILD

SUPPLEMENTAL
REPORT OF LABORATORY EXAMINATION
July 7, 1990

DIAGNOSTICS

Captain Dennis Veach
Columbia Police Department
600 E. Walnut
Columbia, Missouri 65201

Re: Cellmark Case No. F891488
    Your Case No. 89018995

Cellmark Diagnostics
20271 Goldenrod Lane
Germantown, Maryland 208
Telephone (301) 428-4980
800-USA-LABS
Fax (301) 428-4877

It was stated in the Report of Laboratory Examination dated February 15, 1990 that the DNA banding pattern obtained from the semen stain contained the DNA banding pattern obtained from the whole blood labelled Norman Wickizer. Using analysis specific to MS1 & MS31, the frequency in the Caucasian population of the DNA banding pattern common to the semen stain and the whole blood labelled Norman Wickizer is approximately one in 6500. Further testing is ongoing that may provide additional statistical information.

Robin W. Cotton, Ph.D.
R&D Laboratory Manager

Daniel D. Garner, Ph.D.
Directory of Laboratories

FIGURE 2.25 The DNA evidence was crucial in this case. This is the report from Cellmark Diagnostics.

girl screaming. Christine Dampier testified that Wickizer was at home around 6:30 p.m. before Arnold had heard the screaming.

The bulk of the defense's case was spent attempting to create doubt as to the validity of the DNA evidence presented by Cellmark. The defense called as their witness Dr. Moses Schanfield of the Analytical Genetic Testing Center. On direct examination, Dr. Schanfield offered his expert opinion that both tests should have been determined to be inconclusive under Cellmark's own matching criteria and that under Cellmark's criteria, there was no match.

The prosecution was struck by the fact that Dr. Schanfield continued to repeat the phrase "under Cellmark's own matching criteria." On cross-examination, the prosecutor asked Dr. Schanfield if his own laboratory's matching criteria was different than Cellmark's and he stated that it was. He then asked if Cellmark's criteria was more conservative than that of the Analytical Genetic Testing Center, and the expert stated that it was. Finally, the prosecutor asked if the results from the Cellmark tests would have been considered a match if his laboratory's criteria had been used. Dr. Schanfield admitted that the results of both tests would have been considered matches using his own matching criteria.

In the closing argument, the defense stated that the only direct evidence of Wickizer's involvement in the crimes was the DNA evidence. The defense further argued that not only were the results inconclusive, but even if taken as accurate, they only limited the possible assailants to nine men in Boone County, not to mention any number of men passing through town.

In response, the prosecutor asked the jury how many of those nine men were well known enough to the victim to be able to lure the five-year-old who was wary of strangers into the woods? And, how many of the nine men directed the searchers to the area of the body? And, how many of the nine men discovered the victim's well-hidden clothing in an evergreen tree? And, how many of those nine men were in the woods where the body was found from 2:00 until 4:30 p.m. on the afternoon the victim was last seen alive at around 3:00 p.m.? Finally, the prosecutor asked how many of those nine men made numerous statements about what he was doing during the time the victim disappeared which matched exactly the sexual assault that Ramia suffered?

After two hours of deliberation, Judge Hamilton found Norman Wickizer guilty as charged. He sentenced him to life imprisonment without parole for murder in the first degree and nine year's imprisonment for forcible rape with the sentences to be served consecutively.

Wickizer is presently serving his sentences in the Missouri Department of Corrections.

CASE 3

Murder in the Convenience Store

THE SCENE

Joint Communications of Columbia, Missouri, received a 911 call at 1:12 a.m. on February 13, 1994. The call came from the son of Mary Bratcher, manager of the Casey's General Store on Ballenger Lane. Mary's son was concerned because his mother was two hours late coming home from closing the store. Deputy John Gordon of the Boone County Sheriff's Dept. responded to the call. When Deputy Gordon arrived at the store, he saw two cars in the parking lot. He later learned that one of the cars belonged to Mary Bratcher and the other belonged to an employee, Mable Scruggs. Deputy Gordon approached the store's front door and noticed smeared blood around the lock. The door was locked and there was no movement in the building. There was no response to knocks on the door. He radioed for assistance and waited for an off-duty employee to bring a key to unlock the door (Figs. 3.1–3.3).

Several officers, including Steve Brown of the Columbia Police Dept., responded to Deputy's Gordon's request. Officer Brown and other officers began a sweep of the premises. They proceeded cautiously because they didn't know if a suspect might still be in the store.

CASE 3 — MURDER IN THE CONVENIENCE STORE

FIGURE 3.1 This is the scene of the crime.

FIGURE 3.2 The front door was the only access to the store from the outside. It was locked when the officers arrived.

CASE 3 — MURDER IN THE CONVENIENCE STORE   71

FIGURE 3.3 There was smeared blood (arrow) near the lock on both the inside and outside of the front door.

During their search, an off-duty employee of the store arrived with a key. Brown entered the store and quickly checked the large, open customer area. Finding no one in the customer area, he moved towards the employee area at the back of the store, noticing that the cash register was open and next to the counter on the floor, the safe was open as well (Figs. 3.4–3.7).

Through the swinging door labeled "Employees Only", Officer Brown glimpsed evidence of a serious crime. There was blood on the floor in front of the restroom door. He pushed the restroom door open and faced the bodies of two women. Directly to his left, Mary Bratcher, the 46-year-old manager, was lying on her back. The body of Mable Scruggs, an employee, was wedged between the wall and the toilet on the other side of the room. Officer Brown quickly left the bathroom and headed down the hall. He noticed more blood on the floor leading to the walk-in cooler where beverages were stored.

The walk-in cooler was at the end of the short hallway, adjacent to another hallway leading to the back door. There was blood on the

72   CASE 3 — MURDER IN THE CONVENIENCE STORE

FIGURE 3.4 The door to the employee area was to the right after entering the front door. The main counter with the cash register was adjacent to the safe.

FIGURE 3.5 The floor safe had two ompartments, one required a key and the other had a combination lock. Both had been opened.

CASE 3 — MURDER IN THE CONVENIENCE STORE

FIGURE 3.6 The back of the counter shows the safe and the register.

FIGURE 3.7 The register was discovered open. All of the paper money had been removed.

cooler door and handle. Officer Brown carefully opened the door and encountered the body of the third victim, 58-year-old employee Fred Jones, lying near the rear of the cooler. His head was covered in blood and there was abundant blood spattered on the shelves, walls, and floor.

After Officer Brown verified that the three individuals he found were dead and there were no suspects in the building, he returned to the parking lot. He cordoned off the store with yellow police evidence tape and waited for the other law enforcement officials to arrive. At approximately 2:00 a.m., Officer Mike Himmel, a specialist in evidence recovery and crime scene analysis, arrived and took command of processing the site. Over the course of the next few days he would take over 1000 still photographs and hundreds of feet of crime scene video.

As a general rule, a scene is processed from the perimeter towards the body or bodies, and this scene was no exception to the rule. Officer Himmel and his assistants began by videotaping and taking still photographs of the exterior of the store and its location. There were no signs of forced entry and the store's alarm had not been activated; however, as Officer Brown noted, there was blood on the door around the lock on both sides of the front door. After processing the outside and the entryway, the officers entered the store. Except for the area of the counter and the safe, most of the customer area of the store contained little of evidentiary value. A few items on the store's shelves had been knocked on the floor, but this had little to do with the murders.

The open cash register drawer contained a few one-dollar bills, change, and some food stamps. The register display showed $6.31. The tape was still in the register and read 11:02 p.m., 2/12/94. The store normally closed at 11 p.m. A coil of register tape for the day was sitting beside the register, and the last sale was at 10:58 p.m.

On the counter near the register tape roll lay two clipboards. One included a shift audit sheet used by employees to record the monetary business activities of the particular shift that they worked. The top page on the clipboard was Mable Scruggs' sheet. The date on the sheet was

February 12 and the shift she worked was from 5:00 to 11:15 p.m. that day. The remainder of the entries normally made on the audit sheet by closing employees at the end of their shift had not been completed.

Near the clipboards on the counter, Officer Himmel located a small amount of blood and a blood smear. He found more blood smears in the area behind the counter on the floor. In the area between the safe and the front window of the store, he discerned a single set of bloody shoeprints.

One of the department's captains released information about the causes of death very early during the scene evaluation. He surmised that the victims must have been killed with a shotgun because of the tremendous injuries to their heads and the profuse amount of blood at the scene. He reported to the media later in the morning that a shotgun was involved in the murders. However, the crime scene technicians did not adhere to this theory because there was a conspicuous lack of shotgun pellets anywhere around the bodies.

The scene in the restroom was the most gruesome. The two female employees suffered massive head wounds. Blood spatters stained the ceiling, walls, floor, and fixtures. Himmel's close scrutiny of the blood spatter patterns on the walls and ceiling revealed that many blows had been delivered. There were numerous blood droplets on the bottom of the sink which indicated that the victims were down and not moving while blows were being delivered. The injuries to the victims were so extensive that bone fragments and even dentures littered the bloody floor. A .25 caliber cartridge lay partially hidden under the bathroom door (Figs. 3.8–3.13).

Investigators discovered another bloody shoeprint in the hallway in front of the restroom door, this one containing a "Nike" imprint. The door to the walk-in cooler at the end of the hallway was spotted with blood. Inside the cooler was the body of the third victim, Fred Jones. He was lying mainly on his right side in the back, left corner of the cooler. The left side of his head was facing upwards and revealed wounds similar to the head wounds of the women. Officer Himmel

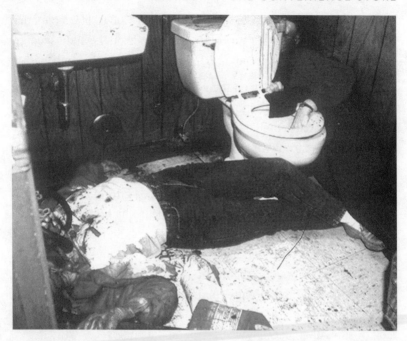

FIGURE 3.8 The two women victims were in the restroom. Blood spatters and pools of blood were on the floor, walls, ceiling, fixtures, and the bodies.

FIGURE 3.9 There were blood spatters on the ceiling of the restroom.

FIGURE 3.10 Blood spatters and smearing on the wall. The patterns of the blood spatters indicated multiple blows to the head and throw-off from the weapon (hammer).

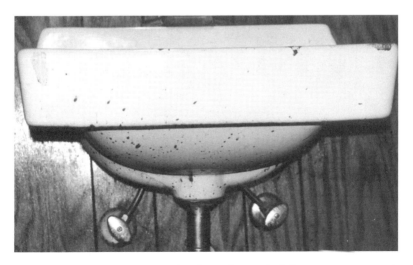

FIGURE 3.11 Blood spatters under the sink revealed the victim was struck numerous times when she was down on the floor.

FIGURE 3.12 In the pool of blood on the restroom floor were bone fragments of the skull (arrows).

FIGURE 3.13 A .25 caliber shell casing was found under the restroom door

CASE 3 — MURDER IN THE CONVENIENCE STORE

thought the height and angles of the blood spatters on the wall above the victim's head proved he had also been struck numerous times as he was lying still. Brain material was visible through the open fractures in his skull. There was no blood on the soles of Mr. Jones' shoes. In fact, there was no blood on the soles of any of the victim's shoes. This made it easy to eliminate any of the their shoes as causing the bloody shoeprints (3.14–3.19).

Later in the evening, members of the medical examiner's office removed the bodies and transported them to the morgue. The autopsies would be completed the next day. The scene examination was not yet complete because the areas around and under the bodies had to be processed for clues. Interesting discoveries were yet to be uncovered.

FIGURE 3.14 This is the view down the hall from the bathroom to the walk-in cooler. There was smeared blood and a bloody shoeprint on the linoleum.

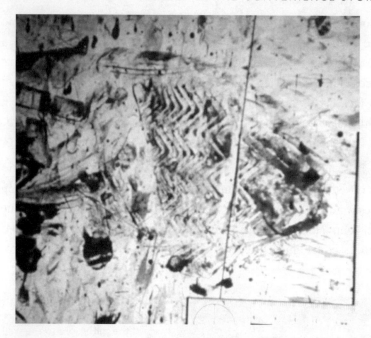

FIGURE 3.15 A bloody shoeprint on the floor was matched to Ernest Johnson's Nike shoes.

FIGURE 3.16 The body of Fred Jones was discovered in the cooler behind these beverages.

CASE 3 — MURDER IN THE CONVENIENCE STORE

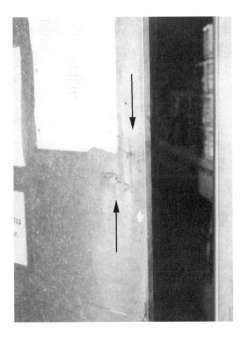

FIGURE 3.17 There was blood (arrows) on the door to the walk-in cooler.

FIGURE 3.18 Fred Jones' body was at the back of the cooler.

FIGURE 3.19 There was abundant blood on the walls, soda containers, and his clothing. There was no blood on the bottom of his shoes.

Himmel discovered a ruptured soda can containing a spent .25 caliber bullet under Fred Jones' head. He also found a .25 caliber shell casing in the cooler. Small multi-dot patterns of blood in both the cooler and at various locations throughout the store were consistent with blood dripping off hands or gloves. Not surprisingly, investigators later recovered a bloody pair of gloves which were worn by the assailant as he carried out the murders (Figs. 3.20 and 3.21).

The medical examiner, Dr. Dix, arrived on the scene before noon on the day the bodies were discovered. He briefly examined the bodies and the scene. After hearing that the police had released to the media the information that the employees were killed with shotguns, Dr. Dix expressed his surprise to Himmel. He also agreed with Himmel that the

FIGURE 3.20 Fred Jones' head was lying on a box containing soda cans.

FIGURE 3.21 A bullet was found in one of the soda cans in the container.

lack of pellets at the scene negated the possibility of a shotgun as the murder weapon. Dr. Dix informed the media he would not render an opinion as to the causes of death until the autopsies had been performed.

THE AUTOPSIES

The autopsies were performed at 8:15 a.m. the next morning by Dr. Dix. Fred Jones was the first to be examined, followed by Mary Bratcher, and finally, Mable Scruggs. Officers Mike Himmel and Bob Brown of the Columbia Police Dept. were assigned to take photographs during the autopsy and to receive any evidence which might be discovered on the bodies (Figs. 3.22).

Fred Jones

The autopsy revealed that Mr. Jones had been shot in the right side of the face with a small caliber weapon. The bullet entered his face above the mouth, passed through his cheek, exited the face near the earlobe of his right ear, and then passed through the earlobe. The gun was fired at least two to three feet away from the body because there was no gunpowder around the entrance wound. The wound was relatively superficial and did not cause any significant damage. It would not have contributed to the victim's death (Figs. 3.23 and 3.24).

Mr. Jones died from multiple blows to the head, especially on the left side. The exact number of blows could not be determined because of the massive damage to the head. There was an open defect (3 and 1/2 inches) on the side of the head involving the left eye and the forehead. There were tears of the skin, brain, and muscle, as well as many fractures of the skull. Besides the open defect there were at least eight more separate blows to the head and left ear. Some of the fractures of the skull were circular, suggesting a hammer as the weapon. In addition, there were two sets of puncture wounds adjacent to the nose. These wounds were consistent with those made by the claw side of a hammer head.

FIGURE 3.22 The three victims: Mable Scruggs (left), Mary Bratcher (center), and Fred Jones (right). (Photos courtesy of the Columbia Daily Tribune).

The other findings of note were lacerations of the three fingers on the left hand and the ring finger of the right hand. There was an impressive fracture of the left ring finger that might have been caused by the finger being caught in the cooler door as it was slammed shut.

Mary Bratcher

Ms. Bratcher also had many blunt impact injuries to her head. The injuries were more spread out over her head than those to Fred Jones. On the back left side of her head were at least four separate blows in one area and an indeterminate number in an adjacent location. She had an open gaping defect (4 by $1^{1}/_{2}$ inches) on the left side of the head. This wound extended from the ear to the forehead. There were other lacerations around the eyes, especially the left eye, and on the neck and forehead. All total, there were over 20 separate individual blows to the head. There were associated fractures of the upper and lower jaw, nose, left cheekbone, and skull. The brain was also torn.

Besides the blunt head trauma that caused death, there were multiple bruises and lacerations of the hands and arms. There were ten stab wounds in the back of the right hand, eight of which went through the hand. The wounds were consistent with those caused by a flat-headed screwdriver and probably occurred as Mary Bratcher raised her hand in a defensive posture (Fig. 3.25).

CASE 3 — MURDER IN THE CONVENIENCE STORE

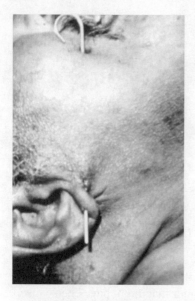

FIGURE 3.23 Fred Jones had a nonfatal gunshot wound to the right cheek. The probe illustrates the path of the wound.

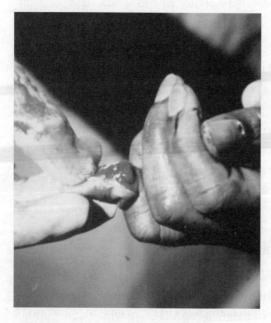

FIGURE 3.24 A fracture of the ring finger on Fred Jones' hand suggested his hand was caught in the door to the walk-in refrigerator.

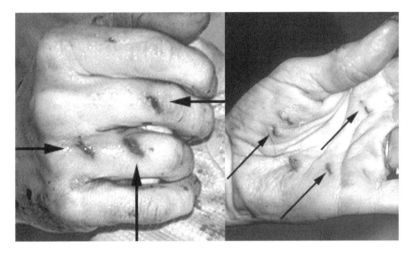

FIGURE 3.25 There were ten screwdriver stab wounds to the hand of one of the victims. Eight of the wounds traveled through the hand.

Mabel Scruggs

Like the others, Ms. Scruggs was killed from being struck in the head. She had a gaping wound on the left side of her head from an indeterminate number of blows. There was a depressed skull fracture on the left side of the back of her head in addition to lacerations of the face and nose. Her nose was fractured. She had been struck more than fifteen times.

The only injury not on her head area was a bruise on the back of her right little finger.

Drug screens were performed on all three victims. The only substances present in their blood were caffeine and nicotine.

Many of the lacerations on the head were semicircular. This pattern strongly suggested a hammer as the instrument of death. At least two of the victims had circular fractures of the skull that implicated a hammer as the weapon. The claw mark puncture wounds to Fred Jones' face confirmed a hammer was used. At the time of the autopsies, a hammer had not been located. The final conclusion was that a hammer was the instrument of death, although both a gun and a screwdriver had also been used in the murders (Figs. 3.26–3.29).

There was no physical evidence from any of the bodies that directly linked any of them to their assailant.

INVESTIGATION

The Major Case Squad, a group of police and deputies from surrounding counties, was assembled on February 13. With this added manpower, many different leads could be followed at the same time. The group's first goal was to thoroughly search the land and neighboring yards surrounding the store. Besides a visual search of the area, there was enough manpower to canvas the surrounding homes. This approach allowed leads to be followed at the same time personnel were involved in a search for evidence. This concentration of manpower led to valuable clues and evidence within a day after the crime.

Across the road from the store was a large open field. Deputy Tom Reddin of the Boone County Sheriff's Dept. organized the search of this field. This effort yielded valuable results, for officers discovered two bloody screwdrivers, a bloody tissue, brown, bloodstained work gloves and a garbage bag of clothes, some of which was spattered with blood. One of the screwdrivers had a flat head and the other a Phillip's head. The one with the flat head contained blood on the shaft. This blood was later matched to that of one of the victims. One of the gloves contained a hair that was later examined and found to be consistent with the hair from one of the victims, Mable Scruggs (Figs. 3.30–3.33).

Adjacent to the field was Indian Hills Subdivision. This subdivision had a park that was also searched. Officers discovered a .25 caliber handgun and a bag of ammunition in the park the day after the murders.

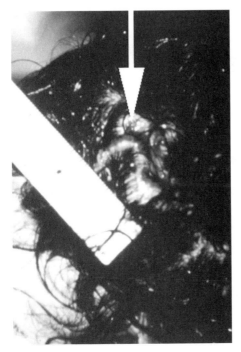

FIGURE 3.26 Semicircular tears (lacerations) of the scalp on one of the victims were consistent with hammer blows.

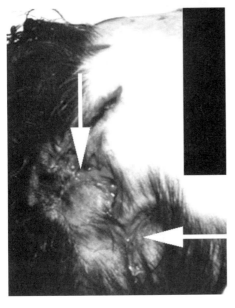

FIGURE 3.27 There were similar lacerations on the other victims.

CASE 3 — MURDER IN THE CONVENIENCE STORE

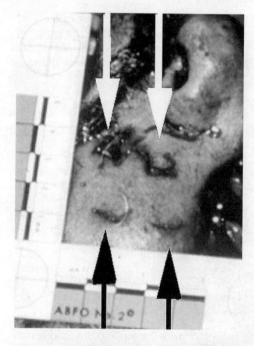

FIGURE 3.28 The arrows point to the wounds caused by the claw side of the hammer.

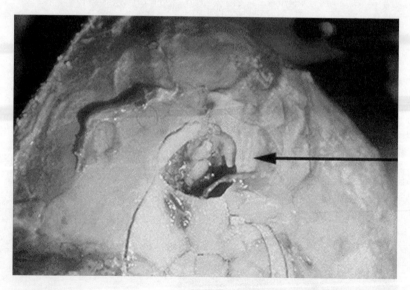

FIGURE 3.29 The arrow points to a classic circular depressed skull fractures caused by a hammer.

CASE 3 — MURDER IN THE CONVENIENCE STORE

FIGURE 3.30 This aerial photo show the store (arrow) and the field across the road where evidence was discovered. 200 Mohawk is in the upper left of the photograph.

FIGURE 3.31 Law enforcement personnel searching the field across from the store.

FIGURE 3.32 This screwdriver was discovered in the field.

FIGURE 3.33 This shoeprint, found in the field, matched Ernest Johnson's Nike shoes.

While the field was being searched, a team of officers converged at 200 Mohawk in Indian Hills Subdivision to follow up on a lead that Ernest Johnson had been seen in the area of Casey's on the day of the murders. At this time he was not considered a suspect. Delores Grant, head of the household, and three children, Rodriquez Grant, aged 18, Antwane Grant, aged 16, and Marcus Grant, aged 13, all lived at 200 Mohawk. Delores Grant was the estranged girlfriend of Johnson who had lived at that location sporadically and kept some of his belongings there. At the time of the murders, Johnson was still residing at Grant's house, but she had asked him to move out.

Ernest Johnson didn't want anything to do with the police when they first arrived at the house on Mohawk. Corporal Jim Mays of the Missouri State Highway Patrol entered the house alone. The eldest son, Rodriquez escorted Corporal Mays to a back bedroom where Johnson was located because Johnson didn't want to come out to the living room. Ernest denied any knowledge of the murders when questioned by Mays. Corporal Mays told Johnson he was not a suspect at this time; the police just wanted to talk to him because he was seen at Casey's the day of the murders. Mays convinced Johnson to accompany him to the police station. Ernest was not arrested or handcuffed.

THE INTERROGATION OF ERNEST JOHNSON

The questioning began at the Columbia Police Dept. at 4:15 p.m. the day after the murders. The interview lasted until 4:20 a.m. the next morning. During this time Ernest Johnson was given breaks including a four-hour nap, use of the restroom, and food.

Johnson said that on the morning of February 12 he had visited his girlfriend, Delores Grant, at a local hair salon. According to Johnson, she had later left town, and he returned by bus to her house in Indian Hills where he had been staying. He departed the bus at the stop nearest to the subdivision: Casey's Store. He then walked over to the residence at 200 Mohawk.

Admitting that he did go into Casey's when he got off the bus to purchase gum and cigarettes, Johnson stated he did not leave the Mohawk residence for the rest of the evening. He locked the door to his bedroom and watched a basketball game, and at approximately 10:30 or 11:00 p.m. he went into the living room and watched television. At about 11:30 p.m. there was a crash that he thought was his waterbed, but he didn't check it out.

There were numerous detectives who took part in the interrogation throughout the night. One veteran, Detective Randy McMillen, confronted Johnson with information he'd received about him being seen in the vicinity of Casey's at approximately 10:30 p.m., near the the time of the homicides. Johnson denied being around the store at that time. During the interview, Johnson did say he had applied for a job at Casey's but that Mary Bratcher, the manager, didn't hire him.

As the interview progressed, Detective McMillen was periodically provided with new information by different detectives working on numerous leads. McMillen was able to keep using this information so the interview could progress smoothly without interruption. Each new piece of the puzzle was used to confront Johnson, keeping him off balance because of his inconsistent statements.

At approximately 6:00 p.m., Detective McMillen was advised that the Grant brothers, Rodriquez and Antwane, had told other officers that Johnson had left 200 Mohawk late in the evening and returned at approximately 10:30 p.m. with a couple of beers. Caught in this lie, Johnson admitted he had purchased the beer; however, he said he had made the purchase earlier when he was let off at the bus stop. He said the person who sold him the beer was Theresa Campbell, the assistant manager who was working the day of the murders. She confirmed that she had seen Johnson on that day and he did buy beer, but the purchase was made later in the evening.

At approximately 6:20 p.m., Johnson finally admitted he had left the house that night, but he said he didn't leave until 1 a.m.

CASE 3 — MURDER IN THE CONVENIENCE STORE

As evidence began to point to Johnson as the murderer, detectives asked him on numerous occasions if he committed the homicides. Johnson's response was to hang his head, look away, shut his eyes, and softly say he didn't know. However, when the officers kept asking Johnson if he had shot the employees with a shotgun, he was adamant in his response that he didn't shoot anybody with a shotgun. Early on in the interrogation, the officers were still operating under the false assumption that the murders were committed with a shotgun. Not shooting anyone with a shotgun was probably one of the few truths Johnson told officers throughout the entire interview.

Toward the end of the interview, the officers learned of new, damaging evidence. A search warrant served at 200 Mohawk yielded a considerable amount of evidence. Detective Susan Stolz and other officers conducted the search. The dwelling is a single-family house with an upstairs area and a basement. In the master bedroom, Det. Stolz located $443 in a zippered bank bag in the dismantled waterbed, black Nike tennis shoes with red laces that tested positive for blood, and a small handgun. Stolz also recovered a blood-stained wadded paper towel on the top of a trash compactor that was located in the basement. In the compactor were burned fragments of checks, coin rolls, and food stamps. The store number and the date of the murder, were still clearly evident on some of the checks (Figs. 3.34–3.40).

With this new evidence, officers asked Johnson to describe his tennis shoes. He said they were black with red laces, but he said he didn't wear them the night before. He said he had worn the boots he was presently wearing. He was then told that the Nike shoes he had described as belonging to him were found in a closet and they had blood on them. The officers were advised that Officer Himmel was shown the Nike tennis shoes and he determined the shoes matched the bloody shoeprints discovered at the store. Johnson was confronted with this information; however, he stuck with his original story that he hadn't worn the tennis shoes the night before.

Officers advised Johnson during the interrogation that Antwane Grant was leading other officers to the area where he had taken the bloody clothing Johnson had asked him to hide. In a soft voice after hearing this, Johnson's only response was, "I don't care."

Near 3:40 a.m., the investigators had heard enough. They escorted Johnson to the booking room for processing because he had just been arrested for the murders of Mary Bratcher, Mable Scruggs, and Fred Jones. The officers and Johnson passed by a holding cell as they were on their way to the booking room. In the cell was Rodriquez Grant. As Johnson walked by the cell he said, "That boy did not have anything to do with it. None of those boys did."

After the booking process was completed, Johnson, now the defendant, was brought back to the interview room. He spoke with two other officers, Kevin McDonald and Ben White. This interview was only 10-20 minutes long. McDonald asked the defendant about any guns he may have owned. Johnson stated he only had one gun, a .22 caliber semiautomatic pistol. Once again he stated that he didn't shoot anyone. McDonald told Johnson that both Rodriquez and

FIGURE 3.34 This home at 200 Mohawk is where Johnson stayed and evidence was recovered.

FIGURE 3.35 Johnson's Nike shoes were found in the bedroom closet.

FIGURE 3.36 These are Johnson's Nike shoes.

CASE 3 — MURDER IN THE CONVENIENCE STORE

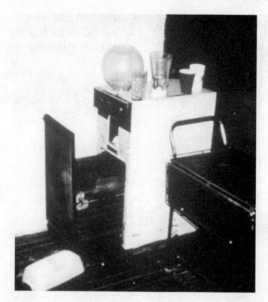

FIGURE 3.37 The trash compactor in the basement contained burned fragments of checks and other items from the store.

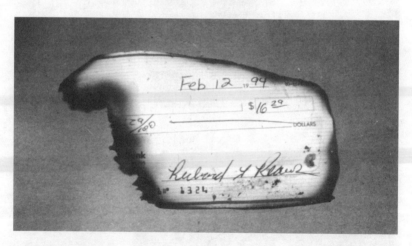

FIGURE 3.38 The date and signature from one of the checks were preserved.

CASE 3 — MURDER IN THE CONVENIENCE STORE

FIGURE 3.39 The waterbed was taken apart and searched

FIGURE 3.40 These are the money and bank bag taken from the store.

Antwane Grant were being arrested for taking part in the murders. At that point Johnson became upset and said, "They weren't there, and I know they weren't there" (Fig. 3.41).

McDonald asked if Johnson knew for a fact that the two young men weren't at the store. Johnson insisted that they were not inside Casey's when the people were killed, not realizing he was implicating himself with his remarks. McDonald stated that the only way that Johnson could know for sure that those two individuals were not there was if he were there. His response was, "I know they weren't there." The officer gathered from these statements that the defendant was alone when he committed the murders.

Assistant Manager Theresa Campbell's interview yielded valuable results. She said she saw Johnson in the store four times on the day of the murders. She knew Johnson quite well, as had all three of the murdered employees. Johnson purchased beer and cigarettes during the late morning. On his second visit, he asked Ms. Campbell, "Who is coming in to relieve you tonight?" She responded that Mable Scruggs would be working and that she, Ms. Campbell, was returning at 11:00 p.m. to help close because it was Mable's first time closing by herself. But Theresa Campbell didn't come back that night; it was Theresa's birthday weekend and Mary Bratcher agreed to work for her. This decision cost Mary her life, but saved Theresa's.

According to Ms. Campbell, the third time Johnson came in, he stayed only a short time and then departed without saying anything. He came in a fourth time toward the end of Ms. Campbell's shift in the evening. On this occasion, he went to the end of the front counter away from the cash register and watched Ms. Campbell make a drop into the floor safe. She was aware that Johnson was observing her. Once she made it clear she had seen him, Johnson left without a word or a purchase.

Interviews with the girlfriends of Rodriquez and Antwane Grant yielded more information about the night of the murders. Around 4:30 p.m. on February 12, Genaya and Debbie Watson arrived at 200 Mohawk. Genaya was the girlfriend of Antwane Grant, and Debbie

CASE 3 — MURDER IN THE CONVENIENCE STORE

FIGURE 3.41 Ernest Johnson is escorted out of the courtroom after his preliminary hearing. (Photo courtesy of the Columbia Daily Tribune.)

was the girlfriend of Rodriquez Grant. Each had a baby by her partner. According to the girls, Johnson purchased crack cocaine from Rodriquez Grant three separate times that evening. The deals were made in the bedroom with the waterbed. The girls didn't actually see the transactions because the door was closed each time.

During the evening, the defendant wanted to know if Rodriquez Grant's .25 caliber semiautomatic Raven pistol was working properly. The defendant, Rodriquez, and Antwane went out the back door of the house where Rodriquez fired one round into the darkness to prove the gun was operational. The gun was missing a clip, so the weapon could only be fired one shot at a time.

Later in the evening, Johnson asked Rodriquez if he could borrow the Raven, and Rodriquez acquiesced. The defendant then departed on foot and alone. He returned shortly afterwards saying, " It wasn't right." He didn't explain what he meant by that statement.

Between 10:00 and 10:30 p.m., the defendant again borrowed the gun and left the house. Genaya Watson noticed that Johnson had changed his clothes from the light or gray sweatpants and lace-up boots he had been wearing earlier. When he left the second time, he was wearing black Nike tennis shoes with red laces, jeans, and a brown canvas coat over a lighter tan jacket with a hood. The hood was up over his head. She also seemed to recall that he was wearing a black turtleneck and dark gloves. When she saw how he was dressed, Genaya joked with Johnson and stated, "You look like you're going to rob somebody; you look like you're going to go rob somewhere." The defendant responded, "I don't do things like that."

An interview with Bart Belgya, who lived in the area, also implicated Johnson. At 10:42 p.m. Mr. Belgya purchased cigarettes at Casey's. This time was confirmed by the register receipt. Mr. Belgya remembered Mable Scruggs waiting on him. As he drove on Ballenger Rd. after leaving the store, Mr. Belgya noticed a thin black man walking down the road toward him in the direction of Casey's. The man was wearing a heavy canvas jacket with a hood over his head.

Chili Lawhorn was babysitting in a house next door to the north side of Casey's. She volunteered that she saw a lone individual matching the defendant's description run across Ballenger Rd. from Casey's toward the field. She didn't know the exact time, but she knew it was late.

Rodriquez and Antwane corroborated the rest of what happened the night of the murders. At 11:45 p.m., the two couples, Debbie and Rodriquez and Antwane and Genaya, walked out the front door of 200 Mohawk. The girls were supposed to be home by 12:00. They left their babies with Marcus while the boys walked the girls to their car which was parked on Comanche Ct. The girls gave the boys a ride back to the Mohawk residence. When the boys arrived home, they noticed Johnson by himself walking into the front yard. Johnson was wearing gray sweatpants, a tan hooded jacket, and the black Nike's. He was not wearing the brown coat and stonewashed jeans that Genaya had seen him wearing earlier.

According to Rodriquez Grant, when Johnson entered the house, Rodriquez and Antwane followed Johnson down to the basement. They watched him remove the gray sweatpants and the shoes which he attempted to clean with a paper towel. Johnson then began to separate the food stamps, checks, and receipts from the cash he had taken from the store. He asked Rodriquez to help count the cash. Rodriquez did as he was told. After setting the checks, receipts, and food stamps on fire, Johnson told Rodriquez to sweep up the charred papers. Rodriquez did so and put the sweepings in the trash compactor. Johnson placed the clothing, except for the shoes, in a garbage bag. Included with the larger articles of clothing were a black Malcolm X tubular hat and a K-State baseball cap. Johnson handed the bag of clothing over to Antwane, commanding him to hide it (Figs. 3.42).

FIGURE 3.42 Antwane Grant led police to these clothes. Johnson asked him to dispose of them after the murders.

Rodriquez and Antwane both noticed blood on Johnson's face and clothing when he was in the basement.

The next night, while Johnson was being interrogated, Antwane Grant took Officer Ken Hammond to the place where he hid the garbage bag of clothing given to him by the defendant. This bag contained a tan coat, green sweatshirt, and gray sweatpants. There were many spots of blood on the coat and a few spots of blood on the cuffs of the sweatshirt.

According to Marcus Grant, the next day at approximately 1 p.m., he and Johnson called a cab that picked them up and took them to the Columbia Mall. They visited two jewelry stores, JC Jewelers and Hurst's Diamonds and they bought several items of jewelry with some of the stolen cash. Johnson gave Marcus more of the stolen cash to keep. They returned to 200 Mohawk and shortly thereafter, the defendant demanded that Antwane Grant hide the .25 caliber Raven and the ammunition. Antwane hid the gun and ammunition in the park next to the subdivision (Figs. 3.43).

On February 15, during a further statement to the police, Antwane Grant led officers to the hiding place in the park. The gun, complete with live ammunition, was identified as Rodriquez's Raven. The magazine was missing. The weapon was sent to the Highway Patrol Lab where it was test fired and proven to be the gun that fired the bullet matching one of the casings discovered in the bathroom and cooler at Casey's.

On February 21, nine days after the murders were committed, the hammer used in the crime was discovered under a crate in the hallway leading from the cooler to the back door. According to the store manager, the hammer was normally kept in a box under the counter near the register. Blood and hair was found on the head of the hammer. The blood on the hammer was later identified as being consistent with the blood of Fred Jones and Mable Scruggs, and the hair was consistent with that of both of the women victims (Figs. 3.44).

FIGURE 3.43 This is the .25 caliber Raven used to shoot Fred Jones.

FIGURE 3.44 This hammer used in the murders was discovered in the back hallway under a crate.

After giving his statement to the police, Rodriquez Grant was charged with aiding and abetting Johnson by giving him the gun he later used in the robbery and murders at Casey's. He was also charged with felony murder. Rodriquez later entered a plea of guilty to the robbery charge, and in exchange for his testimony, the state recommended ten years in prison.

Antwane Grant was a juvenile when the events in this case took place; however, he was certified as an adult. He was charged with two counts of tampering with evidence, the first for hiding the clothing in the trash bag, and the second count for hiding the gun and ammunition. In exchange for his statements, the state dismissed those charges.

THE TRIAL

The Guilt Phase

The state had no trouble producing abundant evidence to prove Ernest Johnson's guilt. The testimony of both Rodriquez and Antwane Grant was crucial. For pleading guilty to lesser crimes, the two men told the court all that they could about the night of the murders (Fig. 3.45).

FIGURE 3.45 This aerial photograph of the field showed the jury the locations of the discovered evidence.

CASE 3 — MURDER IN THE CONVENIENCE STORE

Mike Himmel, the crime scene technician who was an expert in blood spatters, explained the meaning of all the blood patterns and spatters discovered at the scene to the jury. His detailed explanations and photographs gave the jury the most complete picture of what happened to the victims. Officer Himmel explained how many of the blows with the hammer were delivered after the victims were already helpless on the floor. Blood spatters on the walls and ceilings illustrated the movements of the hammer as the blows were delivered. He also showed photographs of the victims' shoes, especially the soles without blood, indicating none of the victims had walked through any blood.

The clothing Johnson wore when he murdered his victims was important evidence. A mannequin was brought into the courtroom and dressed with Johnson's clothing. The location of the blood spatters on the canvas coat suggested the coat was closed and the murderer must have used his right hand to swing the hammer. The jacket, which Johnson wore underneath the coat, had blood only on the cuffs. The blood on the hood of the jacket showed the hood must have been up at the time of the murders (Figs. 3.46–3.48).

Hair and blood from the clothing, hammer, screwdriver, and brown gloves all proved a connection to the victims. Most of these items were connected to Johnson by statements from others or evidence from the scene. The evidence from the house at 200 Mohawk added much information to the case.

The medical examiner was the last of the state's witnesses. His descriptions of the injuries accompanied by gruesome autopsy photographs helped complete the picture of what had happened in the store. He explained that all three victims died from hammer blows to the head. The gunshot wound to Fred Jones' face was not a cause of death. The medical examiner could not tell who was murdered first, but he did testify that the injuries occurred in the locations where the bodies were found. He also explained how the stab wounds to Mary Bratcher's left hand were probably delivered as she was defending herself.

FIGURE 3.46 Johnson wore layers of clothing. There was no blood on the under layers except for some on the cuffs.

FIGURE 3.47 These are the clothes Ernest Johnson wore when he committed the murders.

The defense team of Ms. Kerrow and Ms. Zembles admitted Ernest Johnson's guilt. Ms Kerrow led the defense during this, the guilt phase of the trial. She readily admitted Johnson committed the crimes of which he was accused. However, she contended that he should not be found guilty of murder in the first degree because he did not deliberate about the murders before they were carried out. She stated that he intended to rob the store because he needed money for

FIGURE 3.48 Blood spatters on the right sleeve and front of the jacket reveal Johnson used his right hand to hold the hammer as he struck his victims.

his cocaine habit. Testimony showed that he had used cocaine three times on the night when he committed the murders. She attempted to show that the heinousness of the crimes was not caused by a person who was thinking in a cool and reflective manner. She contended that no person in his right mind could have committed such horrible acts.

The last and rather futile attempt by the defense to save Johnson was a unique one. Ms. Kerrow attempted to show that Johnson did not act alone. She didn't say he had help with the murders, or that anyone else accompanied him; however, she did imply that Rodriquez Grant played an important part in the crimes. She suggested he had a hold over the defendant because of Johnson's need for cocaine, and therefore, in an indirect way, he contributed to the murders.

The jury had no difficulty finding Ernest Johnson guilty on three counts of first-degree murder.

The Penalty Phase

In the penalty phase, the jury had to decide between death or life in prison without parole. The state brought in many of the same witnesses that it had used previously to emphasize the gruesomness of the crime. Family members of the victims were allowed to testify to the extent of their loss.

The defense wanted to prove that Ernest Johnson was affected by cocaine and he was not acting under his own volition, but rather under that of the drug when the murders were committed. Dr. Watson, a doctor of pharmacy, discussed the actions and effects of cocaine and how it can influence someone who is an abuser of the drug. The defense was limited in what evidence it could present because Dr. Watson had not examined Johnson and therefore could not discuss Johnson's mental state at the time of the murders. He could only discuss in generalities what part cocaine might have played in Johnson's actions. The disorder, known as cocaine intoxication delirium, which can cause impressive psychological and physical problems for the cocaine addict, could not be discussed because Dr. Watson wasn't a physician. Ironically, the defense's failure to put a psychiatrist on the stand to testify for Johnson would be the basis for a later appeal and overturning of the verdict in the penalty phase.

The jury gave Johnson the death penalty for each of the three murders.

Appeal and Second Trial

Johnson appealed the death penalty decision on many points. The ineffectiveness of counsel and improper instructions to the jury are common targets for appeals, and these had little impact on the court. But one point persuaded the Supreme Court to overturn the verdict of the penalty phase. The defense attorney's failure to call a psychiatrist to the stand was something the higher court could not overlook. In the hearing to decide the motions, Dr. Parwatikar, a licensed psychiatrist, testified that he had examined Johnson. He testified that at the time of the crime, Johnson did not suffer from mental disease or defect, but he did suffer from cocaine intoxication delirium, a disorder caused by excessive cocaine abuse. It was Dr. Parwatikar's opinion that this disorder was a contributing factor in Johnson's actions the night of the murders.

During the guilt phase of the trial, Dr. Parwatikar attempted to call Janice Zembles, the attorney who directed the penalty phase for the defense. Zembles had scheduled Dr. Parwatikar to testify but had never contacted him. Although she had intended to contact him, she didn't follow through because she was so busy concentrating on her work with two other capital cases.

Regardless of the reasons for this lack of communication, the Missouri Supreme Court ruled it an oversight and granted a new trial for the penalty phase. This trial took place in March, 1999. Much of the same testimony from the first penalty phase trial concerning the crime scene, Johnson's clothing, blood spatters, and the victims' injuries and causes of death was repeated. The main difference was the testimony of a psychologist for the defense.

The defense brought in Dr. Robert Smith, a psychologist from Cleveland. He testified that Johnson was under extreme emotional distress at the time of the murders, and he had an impaired ability to appreciate the criminality of his conduct. These opinions were based on personal interviews with Johnson's family members and a review of a massive number of written reports and records. During cross-examination, the assistant prosecutor was able to show that Dr. Smith possessed little knowledge of the actual circumstances surrounding the murders.

The state also countered with Dr. Jerome Peters, a psychiatrist from the Mid-Missouri Mental Health Center of Columbia. Dr. Peters testified that Ernest Johnson did not have significant brain impairment at the time of the murders. He rejected Dr. Smith's opinion that Johnson suffered from long term depression and borderline mental retardation.

The jury found the state's case credible and once again recommended Ernest Johnson be given the death penalty for each of the three murders. Ernest Johnson is presently on death row in the Missouri Department of Corrections.

CASE 4

Murder of a Family

Susan Brouk was a 36-year-old, recently divorced mother of two. She lived with her children in a trailer on a one and a half acre wooded lot in the small town of Vichy, Missouri. Vichy lies along U.S Highway 63 about ten miles north of Rolla in central Missouri. Susan worked for a small electronics firm in nearby St. James. Her children, 12-year-old Adrian and 9-year-old Kyle, attended public school in St. James. Adrian was in junior high school and Kyle was in elementary school. Susan knew most of her neighbors and was well-liked in this rural community (Figs. 4.1–4.3).

THE MISSING FAMILY

On January 30, 1998, Joy Lamoine, one of Susan's sisters, picked up Kyle and Adrian at the dentist's office, took them home, and stayed with them because Susan was working the evening shift. She left the family after Susan returned home from work. The following day, Kay Hays, Susan's other sister, called and spoke with Kyle and Adrian. She invited the three Brouks to attend Sunday dinner at 3:00 p.m. on the next day, February 1. Kay would later recall that Adrian had chattered excitedly about going to her first dance Saturday night. Adrian also mentioned that her mother had thrown a teenage hunter off the property and Kay reminded the children to keep the doors locked. The Brouk family failed to show up the next day for dinner at Kay's house.

FIGURE 4.1 The home was a modified trailer.

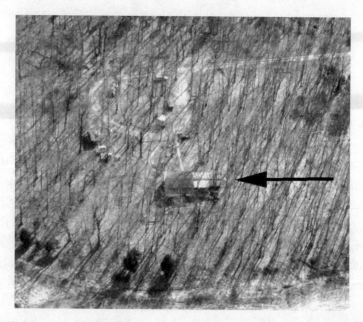

FIGURE 4.2 The Brouk's home was in a rural, wooded area in central Missouri near Vichy, Missouri.

CASE 4 — MURDER OF A FAMILY

FIGURE 4.3 This is an aerial view of the area around the Brouk home.

When Joy learned that Susan and the children had not shown up for dinner at Kay's house, she decided to check on her sister. She called Susan's trailer several times on Monday and Tuesday without success. She also called other family members and Susan's friends to discover her whereabouts. Among those she contacted was David Tackett, a friend who lived in Belle, Missouri. He promised to go by the trailer on his way home from Rolla the next day. After doing so, he reported to Joy that he had found no sign of the Brouks, but he had left a note on the front door of the trailer. By this time it was Wednesday afternoon, February 4, and the Brouks had not been heard from for four days. Deeply concerned, Joy and Kay contacted the rest of the family and they converged on the Brouk trailer. What they found there convinced them that something was terribly wrong. They contacted the Maries County Sheriff's Office.

Deputy Kent Walker received the dispatch from the Sheriff's Office to meet family members at the Brouk trailer in order to complete a missing person's report. When he arrived he found the trailer open and a large number of friends and family members inside. It was clear they had already searched the trailer for some indication of where the Brouks might have gone. It was Joy Lamoine who stepped forward to explain the situation to Deputy Walker.

She pointed out that the family had found the key to the trailer in the lock of the front door and David Tackett's note on the screen door. Another key stenciled with the number 202 was found on the ground nearby, and was later discovered to fit Susan's locker at work. Inside the trailer were other signs of trouble. The family pets, a dog and a cat, had been left unattended in the trailer, obviously for several days. A recently purchased used, tan, Ford Bronco was missing, along with the television and VCR from the entertainment center. Susan's purse was nowhere to be found and the receiver had been disconnected from the phone. Similarly disconcerting, no clothing was missing and both pairs of Susan's glasses were still in the trailer. Susan was extremely nearsighted and wore her glasses at all times. One pair of her glasses was found on a shelf above the bed in Adrian's room. On the floor beside the bed lay a pair of women's panties that were thought to be Susan's because they were too large to have belonged to Adrian.

Deputy Walker, realizing that there was a real possibility of foul play, cleared and secured the trailer. He then called and briefed his superior, Sheriff Doug DiNatali. The Sheriff was quick to see the matter was one that could easily exceed the resources of his small department. He placed a call to Sgt. P. J. Mertens of the Missouri Highway Patrol's Drug and Crime Control Unit. Sgt. Mertens and his partner, Sgt. Ralph Roark, worked out of the Troop I Headquarters located in Rolla, Missouri. They both responded to the call and reached the Brouk residence in 35 minutes.

After talking with family members, touring the scene and discussing the matter with DiNatali and Walker, the two sergeants decided to treat the case as a potential murder. Sgt. Mertens contacted the Highway Patrol's Crime Laboratory in Jefferson City, Missouri, and arranged for a field team to analyze the scene for evidence. Sgt. Roark

CASE 4 — MURDER OF A FAMILY

contacted the air detachment and arranged for a helicopter to conduct an air search the following morning.

It was no secret to any of the officers that the time elapsed since the disappearance of the Brouks, and perhaps since their murders, placed law enforcement at a considerable disadvantage. Gathering forensic evidence at the trailer was a priority. If the Brouks were dead, finding their bodies was crucial if any evidence was to be developed from the scene of the murders. It was also apparent to the officers that no murders had occurred in the trailer. That meant there might be a death scene somewhere else and it was deteriorating with every passing hour. The likely way to tie someone to the disappearance or murder of the Brouks was to locate the Bronco and other property stolen from the trailer. Again, time was working against the officers and they feared the perpetrators may have already disposed of the stolen items.

FINDING THE FAMILY AND THE CRIME SCENE

On the morning of February 5, the helicopter arrived. Sgt. Roark went with Sgt. Word, the pilot, and they began an air search by flying widening circles beginning with the area immediately around the Brouk trailer. In doing so, they flew over the residence of David Bolin and later over several ponds and small lakes located further south and east from the Brouk trailer. The Brouk residence was located near the northwest edge of an irregularly-shaped wooded area which ran to the southeast for almost two miles. Roughly in the middle of this area was the Bolin residence. Along the southeastern edge of the woods was a small farm pond located on the land of Raymond Styles. The officers noticed a brightly colored object in the pond which contrasted sharply with the muddy water and drab winter foliage of the area. Descending low over the pond, Sgt. Roark was able to discern a white shirt and then the face and torso of a white female on the surface of the pond.

After calling for assistance, Sgt. Roark asked the helicopter pilot to land in a nearby field and he walked to the pond. From the bank, the woman's upper body was clearly visible. In the water near the woman's feet were shadows he presumed to be other bodies. After the scene was secured, Sgt. Roark braved the frigid pond water, broke through a thin layer of ice, and pulled what turned out to be the body of Susan Brouk from the pond. He pulled the bodies of Adrian and Kyle Brouk from the shadows near Susan's feet. A cursory examination of Adrian revealed no outward sign of injury except a small, round wound to her upper left arm. Kyle's throat had been cut. Susan's throat had also been slashed. Susan Brouk was dressed only in a bright tye dye t-shirt and gray sweatpants. She wore no shoes or underclothing. Her hands were tied behind her back with yellow, nylon rope (Figs. 4.4–4.10).

An examination of the area around the pond made it clear that this was the place where the murders occurred. Blood spatters were found on the pond bank. There were two sets of footprints, tire tracks, two concrete blocks and an expended 16 gauge shotgun shell located near the bank. The various foot and tire impressions proved of little help to investigators because the soil was saturated from recent rains and print detail suffered accordingly. The shotgun shell was clean and clearly had been deposited there not long before, but there was noth-

FIGURE 4.4 The Brouk family was missing until their bodies were discovered in a pond (arrow) near their home.

CASE 4 — MURDER OF A FAMILY

FIGURE 4.5 The body of Mrs. Brouk was discovered floating in the pond. The children were below the surface.

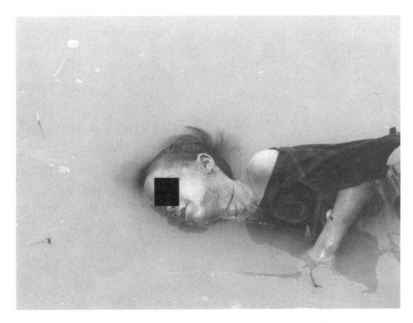

FIGURE 4.6 The children were readily recovered after a brief search. This is the body of Kyle Brouk being pulled from the water.

FIGURE 4.7 The bodies were placed on the bank while the surrounding area was searched for evidence.

FIGURE 4.8 There were no obvious injuries to the Adrian Brouk.

CASE 4 — MURDER OF A FAMILY

FIGURE 4.9 There was a prominent amount of blood on the mother's shirt. Her neck was covered with a piece of clothing that which was used as a gag. This blood came from obvious cutting injuries to the neck. Investigators also saw cutting injuries to the boy's neck.

FIGURE 4.10 Mrs. Brouk's hands were tied behind her.

ing with which to compare it. The significance of the concrete blocks remained unknown (Figs. 4.11–4.14).

FIGURE 4.11 On the other side of the pond was an expended shotgun shell.

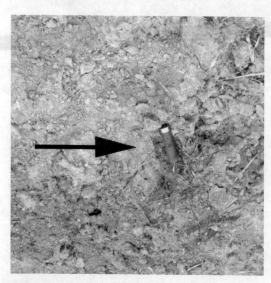

FIGURE 4.12 This is a close-up of the shotgun shell (arrow).

CASE 4 — MURDER OF A FAMILY

FIGURE 4.13 Shoeprints were discovered in the mud; however, they were not used as evidence during the trial.

FIGURE 4.14 There was little blood at the scene, except for these two spots which came from the Mrs. Brouk.

THE AUTOPSIES

The bodies were transported to Columbia for examination. Dr. Dix performed the autopsies of Susan and Kyle Brouk on the afternoon of February 6, and the autopsy of Adrian the next morning.

Susan Brouk

There was abundant blood staining on the outside of Susan's shirt and blood clots under the shirt. There were no injuries or abnormalities to her extremities except for her hands tied around her back. A gag around her face had slipped down over her neck. There were no injuries of the vaginal area. She had two moderately deep cutting injuries to her neck. These slicing injuries did not cut either of the main blood vessels, the carotid arteries, located on the sides of her neck (Fig. 4.15).

The lack of injuries to the genital area eliminated a diagnosis of forcible rape; however, it did not prove she was not raped. The amount of blood on and under her shirt proved that she had been alive and bleeding for more than a few minutes prior to being thrown into the

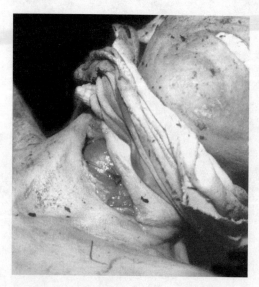

FIGURE 4.15 The cutting injuries to Susan Brouk's neck were deep, although not instantaneously fatal.

pond. The cause of her death was ruled drowning, with the cutting injuries to her neck a contributing cause.

Adrian Brouk

Adrian was dressed in pajamas. Except for a few scratches to her left upper arm, a bruise to the left knee, and a puncture wound to her left upper arm, there were no injuries (Fig 4.16). She was wearing a beaded necklace which left a faint mark on her neck (Fig. 4.17).

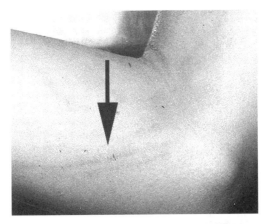

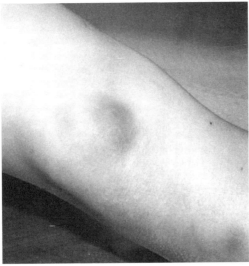

FIGURE 4.16 Adrian also had scratches on the right arm (upper) and a bruise on her left knee (lower).

CASE 4 — MURDER OF A FAMILY

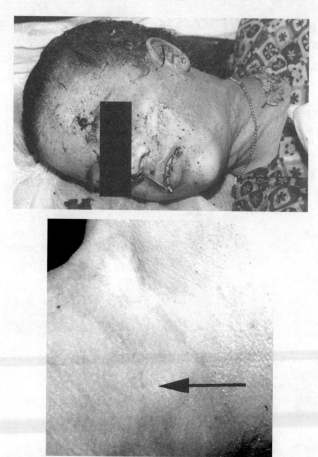

FIGURE 4.17 Adrian was wearing a necklace (upper) which caused insignificant marks on her neck (lower — arrow). There were no injuries in the neck tissues to indicate a manual strangulation

She did have pinpoint hemorrhages, called petechiae, in her eyelids, face, and on the whites of her eyes. Dr. Dix knew petechiae are seen in many different types of sudden death, but they are more commonly seen in cases of strangulation and compression of the chest. Further examination of her neck failed to reveal bleeding in the tissues under the skin which would be expected in a strangulation death. Since she didn't have blood in her neck tissues, the cause of her death was ruled drowning. However, Dr. Dix told the investigators that the presence of the petechiae were not a typical finding in a death due to drowning and the assailant may have suffocated Adrian by compressing her chest prior to placing her body in the water (Figs. 4.18 and 4.19).

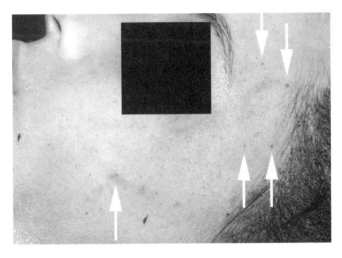

FIGURE 4.18 Adrian had petechiae (pinpoint hemorrhages) of the eyes and on her face (arrows), which suggested that she had been forcibly suffocated by drowning.

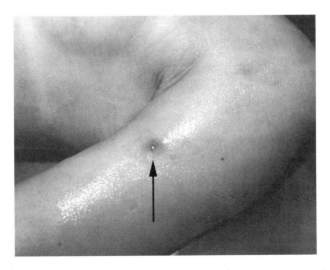

FIGURE 4.19 An injury to Adrian's left upper arm was thought to be from a shotgun pellet.

Adrian also had a shallow puncture wound of the left upper arm. There was no way to prove that this mark was caused by a shotgun pellet, but a pellet could have caused the injury. This question arose because a shotgun shell was discovered at the scene.

Oral, anal, and vaginal swabs of Adrian and Susan were taken and submitted to the lab to for sexual assault analysis.

Kyle Brouk

Kyle was dressed in a t-shirt and jeans. He had two superficial cuts to his neck and a bruise under the scalp. The bruise indicated he had struck something, or he had been hit; the cuts to the neck were not significant enough to cause death. There was no blood on his clothes, indicating there was little bleeding from the neck wounds before he died in the water. The cause of his death was ruled a drowning (Figs. 4.20 and 4.21).

THE INVESTIGATION

After discovering the bodies and analyzing the murder scene, the officers pursued several lines of investigations simultaneously. Sgt. Mertens supervised the processing of the Brouk trailer by a team of criminalists from the Missouri Highway Patrol laboratory. After the bodies were recovered, Deputy Walker recalled that David Bolin had reported on February 1 that his wards, Christeson and J.C., had run away that afternoon and had taken with them two of his shotguns. Walker had filed no report because Bolin refused to press charges. Sgt. Roark entered the serial number and description of Susan Brouk's Bronco into the national crime computer. Sgt. Vislay from Troop F in Jefferson City attended the autopsies and carried the samples taken from the bodies by Dr. Dix to the state crime lab in Jefferson City.

Criminalists at the trailer found little in the way of trace evidence and few usable fingerprints. The search of the trailer the day before by

CASE 4 — MURDER OF A FAMILY

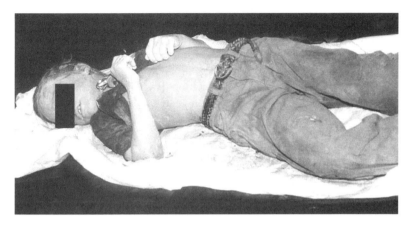

FIGURE 4.20 This is Kyle Brouk's body as seen prior to the autopsy.

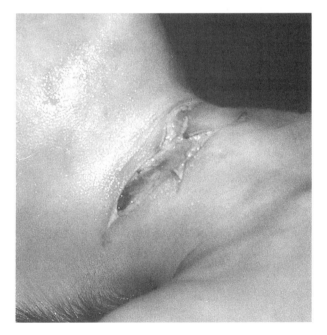

FIGURE 4.21 The cutting injuries to Kyle's neck were not deep. There was a nonfatal blow to his head. He died from drowning.

relatives had thoroughly contaminated the scene. The few samples taken were of questionable value. However, in Adrian's bedroom, serology experts found obvious semen stains on the navy blue sheets of her bed.

Dr. Dix, after performing the autopsies, similarly found little to identify the attacker. He cataloged the injuries and gave samples of blood and other tissues to the officer present. Dr. Dix also took samples from the two female victims according to sexual assault protocols that combined samples of blood, hair combings and samples of oral, anal and vaginal swabs into what is referred to as a "rape kit." These samples were hand-carried by Sgt. Vislay to the Highway Patrol Laboratory for analysis.

Officers contacted David Bolin and spoke with him and other members of his extended family. Mark Christeson and J.C., Mark's younger cousin, lived with their uncle and guardian, David Bolin. (J.C.'s complete name is not given because he had not yet gone to trial for his part in the murders of the Brouk family at the time of this book's printing.) The officers remembered that the previous report of the boys leaving home coincided with the same time the Brouks were last seen.

Mark Christeson was an 18-year-old high school graduate apparently living in his uncle's home, with no steady work and uncertain prospects. He was known to some neighbors for his sullen disposition and reckless driving habits on the gravel roads around the area, but he had no known connection with Susan Brouk or her children. J.C. was a quiet boy who was not well known.

The two boys had cleaned out their room on the afternoon of February 1 and loaded their belongings into a black Oldsmobile which Christeson commonly drove. After being seen driving to the dump area at the back of the property, they told one relative that they were throwing away trash. Later, this same relative checked the dump to see why the young men hadn't returned. He found the Oldsmobile abandoned. Across the fence on the Style's farm, he noticed tire tracks cutting through the field. Curious, he followed the tracks to the county road. When officers examined these tracks, they discovered they passed by

CASE 4 — MURDER OF A FAMILY

the murder scene. In spite of their suspicions, officers could prove only that the two had run away at about the same time the Brouks had disappeared. The boys' connection to the murders had yet to be established.

Later, David and Mary Jo DeLuca would report that they observed a tan Ford Bronco drive past their home and enter their land through a gate about a tenth of a mile from their house. They observed the driver, a tall, thin man dressed in dark clothing, get out of the driver's door and open the gate. He drove through and closed the gate behind the vehicle. The DeLucas then followed the Bronco in their car. They drove down the road and watched the Bronco drive across their fields to a second fence where a passenger left the vehicle and opened a field gate for the Bronco to pass through into the next field. The passenger was shorter than the driver and wore different clothing. While David DeLuca wanted to follow the Bronco, Mary Jo pointed out the vehicle had passed onto the Style's land and it was no longer their concern.

On February 6, Sgt. Roark contacted the Highway Patrol's Information Systems Division and requested they run an off line NCIC (National Crime Information Center) search for Christeson and J.C. Information about wanted individuals and stolen property is available to law enforcement agencies through NCIC. Every inquiry together with the nature of the request is recorded at the center. A computer check through those thousands of inquiries can reveal whether a person or automobile has been checked through the system. In this case, both Christeson and J.C.'s names were the subject of several inquiries in the hours following the disappearance of the Brouks. The first contact was in Shamrock, Texas at 8:04 a.m. central time on February 2. A second contact was made with the two men in Gallup, New Mexico, at 11:37 p.m. mountain time on the same date.

Chief of Police Joe Daniels, a native of Neosho, Missouri, stopped the two men in Shamrock, Texas, following up on the report from the owner of a gas station located near Interstate 44. The owner reported that two teenagers were trying to sell a shotgun or trade it for gasoline.

Chief Daniels found the Bronco in town and spoke with Christeson and J.C. He also took their identification and ran the young men, the guns they had with them, and the vehicle through NCIC. Because no warrants were reported, Chief Daniels was forced to let them go. During his conversation with the two men, Christeson told him the car belonged to his girlfriend. J.C., who was the more talkative of the two, told him that they were desperate for money to buy gas. Daniels provided them with a $5.00 voucher for gas and told them of a pawn shop in Amarillo which was ninety miles to the west. "I knew in my gut there was something wrong about those two, but I had nothing to go on," Daniels would later tell Sgt. Roark.

In McKinley County, New Mexico, Deputy Wayne Robertson came across Christeson and J.C. on February 2. He found them sleeping in the Bronco along the Interstate right-of-way near Gallup, New Mexico. After checking them through the computer, he told them they weren't allowed to sleep on the shoulder of the road. He directed them to a truck stop several miles to the west. Christeson again claimed that the Bronco belonged to his girlfriend, but added that they were bound for Phoenix, Arizona. The Bronco wasn't running properly and had to be push-started.

Sgt. Mertens contacted the New Mexico and Texas police departments in an attempt to gather information about the boys who had suddenly become the primary suspects in the case. After his conversation with Sgt. Roark, Chief Daniels called friends in the Amarillo Police Department, told them which pawn shop he had recommended to J.C., and gave them the serial number and description of the shotgun the two men had attempted to sell in his community. Sgt. Modeina Holmes of the Amarillo Police Special Crimes Unit quickly located the gun at EZ Pawn in south Amarillo. She seized the pawned gun and compact discs, and she recovered the store's copy of the pawn ticket bearing Mark Christeson's signature and the store's surveillance videotape showing the transaction. The unit commander, Lt. Smith, called Sgt. Mertens on February 6, and informed him of their information and the recovery of the evidence. Sgt. Mertens picked up the evidence on February 15. With all this evidence, Mertens and Roark sought warrants for the two men for the murders of Susan Brouk and her children.

Within twenty-four hours of the request, the Maries County Prosecutor filed criminal complaints against Christeson and J.C. for three counts of first-degree murder. Based on the complaints, warrants were issued for the two men directing that they be arrested and held without bond. Information was also sought from the Blythe, California authorities because Christeson was known to have lived there as a youngster.

On the morning of February 9, Detective Jim Lowe of the Riverside, California Sheriff's Department examined flyers concerning Christeson, J.C. and the Bronco they were thought to be driving. He realized that he had seen the two men at a local business the day before while he was off duty. He called the business owner and was told that the two men were working for a local man doing yard work at his home. Lowe secured the assistance of several other officers and immediately drove to the indicated address. As they approached, Detective Lowe saw the tan Bronco parked on the street in front of the residence. Christeson and J.C. were found in the front yard and taken into custody without incident.

Sergeants Mertens and Roark flew to California shortly after being informed of the apprehension of the two suspects. They needed to question the two men and process the Bronco and its contents. The Bronco yielded clothing and property belonging to the suspects as well as property of the Brouk's family. Some of Susan Brouk's papers were also found. The officers next attempted to speak with Mark Christeson; however, Christeson quickly invoked his rights and refused to make a statement. It was later discovered that a Missouri public defender, who did not represent either Christeson or J.C., had called Christeson and instructed him to make no statements to police (Figs. 4.22–4.25).

FIGURE 4.22 This is Mrs. Brouk's vehicle that her killers stole.

FIGURE 4.23 One of the guns used in the crime was recovered behind one of the seats.

FIGURE 4.24 In the glove compartment were shotgun shells similar to the one found around the pond.

FIGURE 4.25 In the back of the truck (upper) was more evidence. Adrian's fishing pole (left) was one of the items discovered.

Public defenders must be appointed to represent indigent defendants. Legally they are not to become involved in a case until a defendant requests counsel. The courts have repeatedly upheld this point of law. Most law enforcement officers also know they must deny a public defender access to a defendant if he has not been requested. But this didn't happen in Blythe because a public defender from Missouri was allowed to communicate with Christeson and tell him not to talk to the police.

J.C. however, hadn't received these instructions about not talking to the police. He eventually confessed to Roark and Mertens about his involvement in the murders of the Brouks. He also implicated Christeson. J.C. had initially denied any knowledge of the murders and presented a rather wild tale of how he had obtained the vehicle by finding it in a field. When confronted with the inconsistencies in his story, he agreed to tell the officers what really happened.

A CONFESSION

According to J.C., he and Christeson had been talking of running away from their uncle's home for some time. It wasn't until the night before they actually fled the state that they decided to carry out their plan. Christeson had an additional agenda however, for he had apparently developed an obsession with an unnamed women who lived on the other side of the woods. He had tried to introduce himself to her, but she had become angry and had run him off. He made it clear that before he left he was going to visit "the bitch who lived through the woods" so he could "have his little fun."

The morning of February 1, the two young men left the Bolin residence at about 10:30 a.m. and made their way through the wooded hills to the Brouk property. Each of them carried a shotgun. Christeson had a 16 gauge which he later pawned in Amarillo, and J.C. had a 20 gauge with a broken stock. At the fence, Christeson directed his

CASE 4 — MURDER OF A FAMILY

cousin to the front of the trailer while he approached the rear. J.C. would later say that he waited so long that he was just about to leave when Christeson opened the front door and waved him inside.

As he entered the trailer, J.C. found the Brouk children sitting on the floor in the living room area and Susan Brouk moving toward them under the muzzle of Christeson's weapon. Susan snapped angrily at Christeson, "This is my house, get out." Christeson directed her to the floor with his shotgun, "You're not giving orders now." He directed J.C. to tie up the Brouks. J.C. did so, using shoelaces brought from home and a piece of yellow rope. He told officers that he didn't know the mother, but he recognized the two children because he rode the bus to school with them.

Christeson told J.C. to watch the kids and directed Susan Brouk to Adrian's room with a terse, "Come with me". J.C. said he could hear squeaks and other sounds which led him to believe that Christeson was having sex with Susan Brouk. When the two returned, Susan was naked from the waist down, except for her sweatpants around her ankles. Because she was still bound with her hands behind her back, J.C. pulled her pants up for her when directed to do so.

Susan, still defiant, told Christeson, "Now you've had your fun, get out." It was at about this time that Adrian said something and called J.C. by name. It was apparent that the children knew their attackers.

Christeson pulled J.C. aside and told him that they would have to "get rid" of the Brouks. This was the first time there had been any mention of murder according to J.C. Christeson and J.C. moved the Brouks at gunpoint to the Ford Bronco which was parked in front of their trailer. Brouk had purchased the Bronco several weeks before, but had never obtained the permanent registration because she lacked funds. The temporary registration had expired and she had stopped driving the vehicle. The lack of license plates didn't deter Christeson; he would later alter the date to make the permit appear valid. He directed the three Brouks into the backseat of the Bronco, commanded J.C.

to guard them and returned to the trailer. He emerged a short time later with the television, the VCR, Brouk's keys and checkbook, compact discs, and other property which they loaded into the Bronco.

Before leaving, Christeson gave the keys to J.C. and told him to lock the trailer. J.C. complied and returned to the front door. He noticed that the door key and one other were attached to the key ring with a separate piece of wire. After locking the front door, J.C. was unable to remove the key from the door. In frustration, he yanked the key chain which broke the wire holding the house key. He left the key in the door. The second key fell to the ground. J.C. climbed into the front passenger seat and Christeson drove away.

Christeson followed a circuitous route from the Brouk trailer over state and county roads, past the DeLuca residence and through a series of field gates to the pond on the Style's farm. Unaware that the Delucas had seen them, the boys ordered the Brouks out of the Bronco and led them to the pond bank.

According to J.C., the Brouks were crying as they herded them to the edge of the water. Susan Brouk, who was at the end of the line closest to Christeson, said something to Christeson which apparently made him angry. He kicked her in the stomach and knocked her to the ground. Christeson ordered J.C. to cut Kyle's throat, but he refused. Then, with the children screaming, "No, no!" Christeson stepped on Susan's head, pulled his fixed blade knife and cut her throat once or twice. Susan continued to move, but the focus of the attack shifted to the children. As J.C. collected concrete blocks, Christeson knocked Kyle to the ground and cut his throat twice. J.C. heard Christeson fire his shotgun as he continued struggling with one of the blocks. He looked up and saw Christeson carrying Adrian to the pond bank.

J.C. said he heard Mrs. Brouk tell her children that she loved them as she lay near them on the pond bank. After dragging Kyle into the water, Christeson held his head under and J.C. held his feet until Kyle stopped struggling. Adrian was next. She was standing on the bank when Christeson tripped her into the water. He grabbed her by the throat in a one-handed choke-hold and held her under water. Again J.C. held her feet until she stopped fighting. The two men then picked up Susan, who was still breathing and threw her into the water with the bodies of her children. The concrete blocks were never used.

After the murders the two men cleaned up the scene as best they could and drove through the fields to the fence across from the dump at the back of the Bolin property. Leaving the Bronco where it was unlikely to be seen they returned to the house and changed out of their muddy clothing. They then proceeded to pack their belongings in trash bags and loaded them through the bedroom window into the black Oldsmobile. They told one curious relative who dropped by unexpectedly that they were cleaning their room and taking trash to the dump. The boys drove the Bronco through the fields to a county road and eventually to Interstate 44 which they followed all the way to California. Along the way they sold property belonging to the Brouks for gas money. Before they reached Blythe they were reduced to begging for money at truck stops. The shotgun and other property they pawned in Amarillo were the last things they were able to sell.

In processing the Bronco, Sergeant Roark found the shotgun J.C. carried, belongings of the two suspects and a variety of property which could be identified as belonging to the Brouks. In particular, Mrs. Brouk's checkbook and vehicle purchase documents were found. J.C. confirmed that the Bronco contained both the defendant's belongings, the shotgun he carried and property stolen from the Brouks. There were also several live 16 gauge shotgun shells in the glove compartment. These shells were of the same manufacture and type as the shell found on the bank of the pond. The two suspects, the Bronco and all the property found in it were eventually returned to Missouri. Many items were submitted to the laboratory for analysis. Of particular interest were the semen samples from the autopsy and the Brouk trailer, and the 16 gauge shotgun and the expended shell.

All evidence in the case was sent to the Missouri Highway Crime Lab in Jefferson City. However, only the ballistic test results were available for the preliminary hearing. The spent shotgun shell found near the pond bank was proven to have been fired from the shotgun pawned by Christeson in Amarillo, Texas. Search warrants had been obtained for blood to be collected from both Christeson and J.C., but test results would not be ready in time for the hearing. The methods used for DNA testing at the time were extremely time consuming. This left prosecutors in the position of having to rely on circumstantial evidence against Christeson who was presumed to be the leader in the murders. J.C. was less problematic because of his statement, but the statement was inadmissible against Christeson unless J.C. testified (Figs. 4.26–4.28).

THE PRELIMINARY HEARING

On April 13, 1998, a joint preliminary hearing was held in Maries County Associate Circuit Court for both defendants. The hearing was held before Judge Gregory Warren of Pulaski County, who had been assigned to hear the case.

Members of the families of both the defendants and the victims were present. There were some harsh words between these two groups and law enforcement officers had to make sure there were no fights. In the end, the concern of the prosecutors that the evidence might be too weak on Christeson was unsubstantiated. The judge bound both defendants over to the circuit court for trial.

In the months that followed, the Christeson case, in no small part due to the efforts of the prosecution, moved toward trial faster than the case against J.C. There were exploratory discussions between prosecutors and J.C.'s attorneys to determine whether he would be willing to testify against Christeson. Those discussions broke down in short order. However, developments on another front were about to change the situation completely.

CASE 4 — MURDER OF A FAMILY

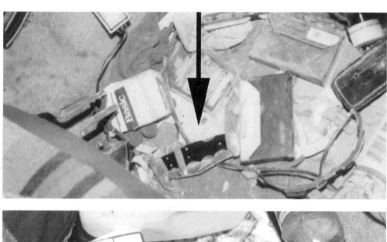

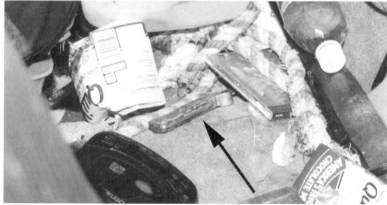

FIGURE 4.26 These knives were discovered in the truck; however, none of them could be linked directly to the murders.

CASE 4 — MURDER OF A FAMILY

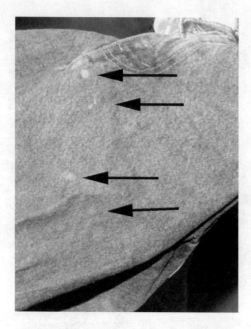

FIGURE 4.27 There were spots of blood on these jeans found in the truck; however, they could not be matched to Mrs. Brouk or the children.

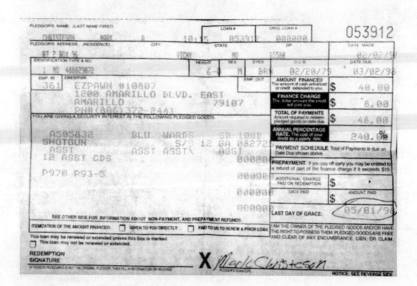

FIGURE 4.28 The shotgun used during the crime was pawned in Texas. This receipt was kept in the truck.

CASE 4 — MURDER OF A FAMILY

The long anticipated lab report concerning the results of DNA testing came out in August, 1998. Serologist Tom Grant of the crime laboratory had found semen on the sheets from the Brouk's home and on the vaginal swabs taken from Susan at autopsy. DNA testing of all the samples took months to complete. Serologist and DNA examiner Cary Maloney had to perform multiple tests, one on the blood of each of the three victims, blood from both defendants, and semen from the two sheets and vaginal swabs. For prosecutors however, the results proved worth the wait. Against the odds, given the delay in recovering the samples, precise results were obtained on the six gene sites probed. The semen on the sheets and the swab contained a gene pattern which was identical to that in the blood of Mark Christeson. Christeson's pattern was quite rare, for it was found in Caucasians only once in 1,320,000,000 individuals. It appeared that Christeson was now tied to the rape of Susan Brouk and, by inference, her murder and that of her children.

It appeared that the trial of Mark Christeson could boil down to a battle of experts on DNA issues. While the courts have long accepted DNA results as scientifically accurate, defense attorneys commonly draw upon a host of paid experts to either denigrate the accuracy of the tests, attack the competence of the examiners, or criticize the practices of the lab in question. During the battles over discovery between the parties prior to trial, it emerged that the defense in this case intended to use a known defense expert, Dr. Dean Stetler of Kansas University. Dr. Stetler was known for his method of attacking lab practices or the procedure used in the particular test the state was expected to rely upon. Prosecutor John Garribrandt and Assistant Attorney General Bob Ahsens therefore expected that the defense would take the position at trial that the defendant, Christeson, did not rape Susan Brouk, let alone kill her, and the test was flawed. The prosecutors began gathering information on Dr. Stetler to demonstrate his bias.

Another issue which arose prior to trial was the admissibility of evidence that Susan Brouk had difficulty with Christeson and J.C. prior to the murder. A neighbor, Sheila Lenhardt had belatedly told investigators that she had seen Susan Brouk the evening of January 31 at a local restaurant and tavern. Susan had spoken with Mrs. Lenhardt for a time. She was waiting to pick Adrian up from her first dance which was being held at the junior high school. Kyle was with her and was playing pool with Mrs. Lenhardt's daughter, Shelly, while the adults talked. During their conversation, Susan described several incidents in which she had found one or more teenagers hunting on her property without permission. As she told it, the incidents left her uneasy.

Susan described the first time she encountered two teenage boys to Sheila. The older of the two was tall, thin and dark; the younger was shorter and fairer. Both were armed with shotguns. She stated she did not allow hunting on her property because of the potential for accidental injury to her children or pets. She asked them to leave. The two boys were sullen but complied with her request. There were two other incidents. One or both of the boys came to the house and asked to use the restroom. She refused to let them into the trailer. On the last occasion they requested use of the telephone. They were armed with the shotguns. Mrs. Brouk said she ordered the two off her land and told them never to come back. She said they became angry and "mouthy" when she told them that if they came back she would call the police. She also instructed her children to keep the doors locked and to call the sheriff if either of the two boys dropped by again.

Susan Brouk described the two young men in detail and Sheila Lenhardt had to admit she didn't know who they were. Susan further stated that she thought the two unwelcome visitors came from "Bolin Hill," referring to the land owned by David Bolin. Shelly Lenhardt, who had overheard the descriptions of the two boys, immediately recognized the two as Mark Christeson and J.C. She said that she rode the school bus with them and that they were the only two living at "Bolin Hill" who fit the description.

Defense counsel sought to suppress much of the state's evidence in the case and in particular any testimony of Sheila Lenhardt concerning what she had learned from Susan Brouk. The defense attorneys argued that the statements were hearsay, with one witness testifying to a statement by someone who is not present in court to testify. The judge ordered such statements to be suppressed. The defense attempted and failed to suppress the DNA results and the samples they were based upon, the ballistics tests and the weapons, and the other recovered property. It appeared that the trial would become a battle of experts over the evidence.

Fourteen days before J.C.'s trial was to begin the entire complexion of the case changed. Although all attempts to obtain J.C.'s testimony had failed up to that time, his lawyers realized that once Christeson was tried they would have no bargaining position remaining for their client. The day before the trial was to begin, J.C.'s attorneys offered his testimony in return for a waiver of the death penalty. This meant that a trial would still take place, but without the death penalty as an issue. This was a concession on the part of the defense who had been insisting on a great deal more leniency up until that time. Prosecutors accepted the proposal. The defense was informed by telephone that evening and in writing the following day. The defense immediately moved for a continuance, insisting that J.C. was not mentally competent to testify. They claimed that they did not have time to prepare for this unexpected change of events.

The Court directed that depositions of J.C. be conducted and that other witnesses be made available for deposition or interview. This was accomplished during the following week. The defense continued to press their request for a continuance and for exclusion of J.C.'s testimony based on his supposed mental problems. The Court found the witness competent to testify, but appeared to be giving a more sympathetic ear to pleas for continuance. However, when the defense indicated they could not again be available for nearly nine months and that the further investigation they required consisted of interviewing J.C.'s former schoolmates, the Court denied the motion.

THE TRIAL OF MARK CHRISTESON

The trial commenced in Nevada, Missouri, on Friday, August 26, 1999, with jury selection. The process moved more quickly than expected and the jury was seated by the end of the day. Opening statements and eight state's witnesses were heard on Saturday. The state's case continued on Monday and into Tuesday morning. The highlight of the case was the testimony of the co-defendant J.C. His testimony was very similar to his original statement to the police. The defense cross-examined him rigorously, emphasizing that his statements were not always the same, implying that he had changed statements because of his plea bargain. However, J.C. disarmed much of this attack by simply admitting he lied to some people to cover up his involvement in the crime. He admitted his guilt and demonstrated a complete lack of guile. In short, he was believable.

By contrast, the defendant took the stand and insisted that he knew nothing of the murders and that the Bronco had been found by J.C. in the woods. Then, to the surprise of everyone in the courtroom, he claimed that he had consensual sexual relations with Susan Brouk on Saturday, January 31. He was unable to explain why Susan Brouk would be interested in him or willing to engage in relations in her daughter's room. Neither could he explain the shotgun shell at the pond or his willingness to take and sell or use property that wasn't his. He tried to explain his flight to California by accusing his guardian, David Bolin, of being a tyrant.

After closing arguments on the afternoon of Wednesday, September 1, the jury retired to consider Mark Christeson's guilt. Approximately three hours later the jury returned verdicts of guilty on three counts of first-degree murder. The penalty phase of the trial began the next morning. The state presented evidence of the defendant's sexual assault on a retarded cellmate in the jail while he was awaiting trial and the testimony of members of Susan Brouk's family concerning the effect the murders had on them. The defense countered with family members of the defendant testifying about his unfortunate upbringing and an expert to testify about the negative impact of that upbringing on the defendant.

After the testimony, the jury retired to decide life or death. Two and a half hours later the jury returned verdicts of death on each count. On October 8, the Court took up the defendant's motion for a new trial or a judgment of acquittal. The defense alleged more than one hundred specifications of error, but argued only three. Those were the motion for continuance, suppression of J.C.'s statement and whether J.C. was competent to testify. The Court overruled the motions and proceeded to sentence the defendant to death on all counts.

Mark Christeson is now on death row in the Missouri Department of Corrections. His partner, J.C., is awaiting trial.

References

1. Columbia Daily Tribune
2. Columbia Missourian
3. Personal Communications
4. Trial transcript – St. v. Ernest Johnson
5. Post conviction motion response – St. v. Normal Wickizer
6. Post conviction motion response – St. v. Ralph Davis
7. Autopsy reports of the Susan, Adrian, and Kyle Brouk.
8. Autopsy reports of Fred Jones, Mary Bratcher, and Mable Scruggs
9. Autopsy report of Ramia Montgomery

About the Author

Dr. Dix is a board-certified forensic pathologist who has been performing autopsies and death scene investigations for over twenty years. He trained at the U. of Missouri-Columbia and the Hamilton County Coroner's Office in Cincinnati, Ohio. He has been the medical examiner for Boone and Callaway Counties in Missouri since 1980, except for a brief stint as the Deputy Chief Medical Examiner for New York City. He has published numerous forensic texts and computer-based atlases. He teaches forensic pathology to medical students and residents and has a class in forensic pathology and death investigation for undergraduate and graduate students. He is married, with two children, and loves his work.